In a solitude of the sea
Deep from human vanity,
And the Pride of Life that planned her, stilly couches she.

Over the mirrors meant
To glass the opulent
The sea-worm crawls — grotesque, slimed, dumb, indifferent.

Dim moon-eyed fishes near
Gaze at the gilded gear
And query: "What does this vaingloriousness down here?" . . .

From Thomas Hardy's
"The Convergence of the Twain" (Lines on the loss of the *Titanic*)
1912

GHOSTS
OF
THE ABYSS

A Journey into the Heart of the Titanic

BY DON LYNCH AND KEN MARSCHALL
Introduction by James Cameron

DA CAPO

A DA CAPO PRESS / MADISON PRESS BOOK
Produced in association with Walden Media, LLC

Produced by
Madison Press Books
1000 Yonge Street, Suite 200
Toronto, Ontario, Canada
M4W 2K2

Printed and bound in Italy

Cataloging-in-Publication data for this
book is available from the Library of
Congress
ISBN 0-306-81223-1

Published by Da Capo Press
A Member of the Perseus Books Group
www.dacapopress.com

Da Capo Press books are available at
special discounts for bulk purchases in
the US by corporations, institutions
and other organizations. For more
information, please contact the Special
Markets Department at the Perseus
Books Group, 11 Cambridge Center,
Cambridge, MA 02142, or call (617)
252-5298.

1 2 3 4 5 6 7 8 9——06 05 04 03

Page 1: A rattail fish
swims by a Dining
Saloon window.

Page 2: The telemotor that
once held the ship's wheel
remains on the bridge.

Page 3: The ghostly prow
of the *Titanic* wreck.

Page 4: A davit for
lifeboat No.1 still stands
on the Boat Deck.

Page 5: Second-class
passengers look over the
railing at the aft end of
A Deck on April 11, 1912.

Page 6: The port anchor
sits above the rusticle-
strewn ocean bottom.

Page 7: Lights from a
submersible illuminate
the A-deck promenade.

CONTENTS

INTO THE HEART
of the TITANIC

No two people in my experience have contributed more to our understanding of the *Titanic* and its tragic sinking than Ken Marschall and Don Lynch. Ken's luminous artwork, based on his unparalleled knowledge of the ship, and Don's encyclopedic mental database of her crew and passengers make them unrivaled *Titanic* authorities. For this reason, I asked them in 1995 to act as advisors on my film *Titanic*. Not only did they help me get it right, but we also became friends in the process. When I began planning a return expedition to the *Titanic* in 2001, I enlisted their aid again. This time, the objective was not merely to photograph the exterior, as we had done during our 1995 expedition, but to use sophisticated remotely operated vehicles (ROVs) to do a thorough imaging survey of the interior of the wreck. My hope was that Don could help me identify which passengers had been in which cabins and prioritize the list of historically interesting targets. Ken, meanwhile, could bring his vast knowledge of the wreck to bear in planning ROV penetrations of the various deck levels, cargo spaces, and so on.

After our initial planning meetings, it quickly became clear to me that these two *Titanic* experts would prove invaluable on the expedition itself — so I offered them the chance to come along. And I'm grateful that they both accepted. *Ghosts of the Abyss*, the film that resulted from the 2001 expedition, clearly demonstrates their contribution to the mission, and we certainly could not have accomplished what we did without their participation.

Ironically, neither Ken nor Don was particularly interested in diving to the wreck itself. Many people are daunted by the prospect of being locked up for sixteen hours in the cramped manned sphere of a deep-sea submersible (a space about six and a half feet in diameter) with 125 million pounds of water pressure squeezing the sphere from the outside as it crawls along the vast ocean floor — searching the pitch darkness with sound waves instead of vision. It's definitely not for the faint of heart. Add to this the hazards of wreck diving — turbulent currents flowing around the wreck that can spin the submersible out of control, or twisted steel that can snag and trap the sub — and you find that most sensible people decline the offer.

But as the expedition progressed, I could see that both Ken and Don were becoming more and more fascinated by the diving itself. And it was clear that they were finding it hard to resist the strong pull that a close-up look at the wreck had on them. Finally, a week into the dives,

both of them made the final plunge — literally!

Ken eventually made four trips down to the *Titanic*, and Don made two. They became hardened sub divers, adept at underwater navigation and communication, and were of great assistance to me in planning and in actually performing the very complex operations on the bottom. Ken's ability to find his way around the wreck was uncanny. I might be piloting the ROV Jake deep inside the wreck, down on the D-deck level, and I would ask Ken in the other submersible to move to a specific porthole — say, D-35 on the starboard side — and shine the sub's spotlight inside. Within minutes, Ken would have directed the sub pilot to the exact window and the light would come bursting in like a sunrise. It was moviemaking magic.

Diving with Don was also a great experience. We might be looking at a spot on the Boat Deck, or at a window or a davit, and Don would always know exactly what had happened there. He was able to tell the story of the *Titanic*'s passengers and crew right there — right at the very spot it happened. To be in that alien place, exploring this vast human artifact, and to have these two historians bringing it to life with their intimate knowledge of the event was for me the pinnacle of underwater exploration. I can only guess what the experience was like for them. In Don's case, to actually witness and interact with the ship that had dominated his work and thoughts for decades must have been amazing. And Ken's endless curiosity about the wreck must have been satiated and simultaneously whetted even further by the images that the two intrepid little 'bots were able to bring back.

Together, we were able to explore many of the interior spaces of the wreck — though others remained tantalizingly out of reach. With the help of the specially designed 'bots, we imaged areas that had never been photographed before and finally found out what they looked like. In 1912, no one expected that the ship would live only a few days, so it was always assumed there would be plenty of time to photograph her inside and out. The *Titanic* went to the bottom with many secrets, and we were able to unveil a few of them. Thanks to Ken and Don's systematic analysis of the images we retrieved, we now understand so much more of the interior architecture and design of the *Titanic*, as well as the events of the sinking.

I was on the bottom of the ocean, at the wreck site along with Ken and Don, when the attack of September 11 took place. We surfaced into a changed world. Our sense of isolation was intensified because we were stuck out in the middle of the North Atlantic, hundreds of miles away from the unthinkable tragedy that had occurred at home — and away from our families and friends. At the same time, everyone on board was drawn closer together, in a bond I suspect will be lifelong.

The 9/11 attacks also made us reassess what we were doing at the *Titanic* site — and why. Here we were, poking through the wreckage of the defining disaster of the early twentieth century, while the defining disaster of a new century had just taken place. At first, our passionate study of the *Titanic* wreck seemed suddenly pointless and trivial — but in the following days, it took on a new meaning. It became a way for us to talk about tragedy and loss, and about the shock and numbness caused by events that seemed out of all human proportion. The *Titanic* was a "safe" tragedy from another century, and we used it to focus our emotions. It helped us come to terms with what was happening in our world now — and perhaps that is ultimately the reason for our collective fascination with the *Titanic*. The disaster has always been the quintessential story of loss, of coming to terms with death, of heroism and cowardice, and the full spectrum of human response before, during, and after a crisis. As such, it will always be with us as one of the great lessons of history. And its mythic status will endure.

Ken Marschall and Don Lynch are among the most gifted bearers of the *Titanic* story, and this book illuminates and continues the legend of the mighty ship.

— *James Cameron*

Berth 44 at the Southampton docks today and (opposite) on sailing day, April 10, 1912.

Chapter One   *The Journey Begins*

Second Officer Charles Lightoller braced himself as a stiff gust of wind whipped against his uniform. It was sailing day — April 10, 1912 — and the Royal Mail Steamer *Titanic* bustled with activity as crewmembers, officers, and suppliers swarmed around her decks, making final preparations for the ship's maiden voyage from Southampton to New York. Carpets had been laid and final decorating had been done right up to the last minute, and the smell of fresh paint permeated the ship.

All the same, Lightoller viewed the scene with some frustration. Before the 46,328-ton vessel could leave England, she had to go through yet another inspection under the eagle eye of Captain Maurice Clarke, the assistant emigration officer under the Board of Trade. It was Clarke's duty to make sure the ship was fit to take emigrants from England, and he had a reputation for being extremely meticulous. Captain Benjamin Steel, Southampton's marine superintendent for the White Star Line, would participate in the inspection, but he was normally quite genial and would likely inspect in a very general way. Clarke, however, would ask for the lifebelts to be brought out and he'd insist that the lifeboats be uncovered and the contents removed. He was

even known to have a lifeboat lowered more than once if he wasn't satisfied the first time.

The *Titanic* had sixteen watertight compartments with doors that could be closed with the flip of an electric switch. If the hull were damaged, those doors would be lowered shut to prevent water from entering other parts of the vessel. But Lightoller knew that no ship was perfect and things could go wrong, even on this marvel of Edwardian engineering.

As Clarke and Steel observed the mustering of the sailors and stewards at 8:00 A.M., Lightoller tightened his square jaw and hoped for the best. Once these men had been mustered, they would be allowed to go back on shore before sailing, where the pubs were crowded with crewmen having one last drink before shipping out, as alcohol was strictly forbidden to them on the liners.

Under the unswerving gaze of Clarke and Steel, a group of sailors was taken over to the starboard side of the windy Boat Deck. From there, two lifeboats were lowered into the water from their davits, the small cranes used to send the boats down to the sea. Fifth Officer Harold Lowe and Sixth Officer James Moody manned one boat each, with eight sailors rowing under their command, and the two officers

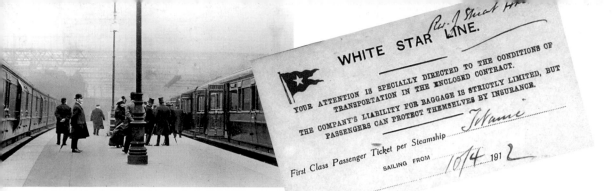

were taken around the harbor for twenty minutes before the boats were hoisted back on board. Normally, inspectors would have had the men set the sails as well, but as Steel later explained, the weather was so gusty that they decided to check only the oars and the sailors' rowing skills.

Also on board for the inspection was Thomas Andrews, the managing director and head of the design department of Harland and Wolff — the Belfast shipbuilding firm that had constructed the *Titanic*. Today, he'd come on board at 6:00 A.M., but during the construction of the ship, he'd been known to arrive in the Belfast shipyards as early as 4:00 A.M. in a bowler hat daubed with paint. Once Clarke and Steel had finished their inspection, they would leave for shore, but Andrews would stay on board to accompany the *Titanic* on her maiden voyage and check for areas that needed improvement.

Not long after the end of the boat drill, a wavy-haired man with a full handlebar moustache appeared on the ship. It was J. Bruce Ismay, the managing director of the White Star Line, who'd motored down from London the day before in his Daimler landaulet touring car with his wife Florence and their three youngest children. Ismay's family would go on to holiday in Devonshire and Wales, but Ismay would accompany the *Titanic* as she traveled to New York, staying in one of the two parlour suites amidships and enjoying his own private promenade deck.

As head of the White Star Line, Ismay had the authority to choose the *Titanic*'s commander. He'd given this honor to Edward John Smith, who, at sixty-two, was the White Star's commodore, or senior captain. Smith had been with the company for over thirty years and had spent the last twenty-five as captain of some of its finest ships. Lightoller would later describe Smith as "full-whiskered and broad" with "a pleasant, quiet voice and invariable smile." Smith was extremely popular with his crew and with the wealthy financiers and upper-class passengers who sailed on his ships. His ease in the company of the rich and famous had gained him a reputation as the "millionaires' captain." Commanding the *Titanic* was the crowning achievement of his long career, and upon his return to England, Captain Smith intended to retire.

By ten o'clock, passengers were beginning to come on board. Excitement over the impending voyage ran high, but there was also a certain amount of confusion. Most were unaccustomed to the enormous size of the nearly nine-hundred-foot-long *Titanic*, and finding their way around was often difficult. The first-class public rooms were open for inspection by second-class passengers, and many took the opportunity to revel in the glamor of spaces that would normally be off limits: the first-class Lounge, decorated to look like the palace at Versailles; the forward Grand Staircase

Other liners could not compare with the White Star's *Titanic* and *Olympic* for the luxuriousness of their first-class accommodations and amenities — including the Lounge (above), with its Louis Quinze–style carved woodwork, and the Turkish baths and swimming pool (insets, left). The third-class lounge (right), though spartan by comparison, still provided a level of comfort for steerage passengers that exceeded anything available to them elsewhere.

between the first and second funnels, which swept down four levels to a white-paneled Reception Room dotted with wicker chairs; and the first-class Dining Saloon with its elegant leaded-glass windows. Nearer the stern, but still on the upper decks, were the Café Parisien and the first-class Smoking Room. On the lower levels, above the boiler rooms in the forward portion of the ship, were Turkish baths and a swimming pool — the second ever to be built into an ocean liner.

Steerage passengers were briefly detained before entering the ship while a Board of Trade health inspector checked their eyes for trachoma and their heads for lice. Either condition would prevent them from being allowed to embark. First- and second-class passengers boarded more freely, then made their way through the maze of corridors and decks to their staterooms. On the dock below, tons of baggage were unloaded from the boat train that had arrived from London and were either brought on board to be placed in the appropriate rooms, or, in the case of bags and trunks that would not be opened during the voyage, transferred to the cargo holds.

At noon, with the help of a swarm of six tugboats, the *Titanic* began to ease away from her berth toward the River Test and the English Channel. From there, it would steam to Cherbourg, on the north coast of France, then to Queenstown, on the south coast of Ireland, before heading out into the open Atlantic. A huge crowd, mostly local citizens, watched from the dock, and some followed the queenly vessel as it moved away from the quay.

The ship turned to port as it entered the narrow channel of the River Test, and as it moved forward, it drew alongside the liner *New York*, which was moored nearby beside the *Oceanic*. Then, as the *Titanic*'s passengers watched, the *New York* seemed to move out toward the *Titanic*, the lines connecting it to the *Oceanic* stretching taut under the strain. As the bows of the *Titanic* and the *New York* came toward each other, the massive lines holding the moored ship suddenly snapped, sounding like gunshots as they arced into the air. The crowd on the dock retreated in alarm as the *New York*'s stern began to swing out into the river, heading straight for the side of the *Titanic*. Men on board the smaller vessel quickly began draping collision mats over the side, while one of the tugs that had cast off from the *Titanic*'s bow now came around her stern and tried to secure a line to the *New York*. On board the *Titanic*, the harbor pilot, George Bowyer, ordered the port propeller forward — an astute move, as it created a sudden surge and a wash that helped keep the smaller liner away. As the *New York* swung out, her bow moved forward, so that her stern actually moved along the side of the *Titanic* and finally passed across the new liner's bow. The two ships missed colliding by only a few feet.

Until the other vessel could be secured, the *Titanic* was stopped in the river. There was considerable excitement among the crowds on the *New York*, the *Oceanic*, and the wharf, but those on the *Titanic* remained calm, the ship's huge size creating a feeling of invincibility. Half an hour later, when the *Titanic* was finally under way again, the *New York* incident was the topic of many discussions, and some passengers expressed misgivings about the maneuverability of this enormous new liner.

As the *Titanic* steamed across the English Channel toward Cherbourg, the waters were remarkably still, a precursor of the calm seas that would surround the ship during the remaining four days of its existence.

(Right) The *New York*, right, is maneuvered to a temporary mooring after its near-collision with the *Titanic*. The *Oceanic* is at left. (Below) A photograph of the *Olympic* on sailing day illustrates what the *Titanic* must have looked like as it eased away from its berth on April 10, 1912.

The *Titanic* was too large to dock at Cherbourg, so passengers at this port were sent out in the White Star tender *Nomadic* and taken aboard in the harbor. Steerage passengers and their luggage were unloaded from a second tender, the *Traffic*. It took an hour and a half to load the passengers and their trunks, including the valuables of many prominent Americans who were going home first class after traveling on the Continent. Among these was one of the wealthiest men in America, John Jacob Astor, the fur trader's great-grandson who had enhanced his inherited riches through clever real-estate deals. After a scandalous divorce and remarriage to Madeleine Force, a woman younger than his son, he had "escaped" with her to Europe. Now he was returning to New York with his new wife, who was five months pregnant. Many third-class passengers — most of them from southern Europe and a good number from Armenia and Syria — embarked at Cherbourg as well.

By 8:30, the last passengers were aboard and the handful who were only traveling cross-channel had disembarked. The *Titanic's* engines rumbled to life, the anchor was raised, and the ship slowly sailed toward its last stop — Queenstown, Ireland. Meanwhile, many of the passengers headed to the dining saloons for a late dinner. Since it was the first night at sea, and as so many had only just come on board, appropriate dress was overlooked. Others, exhausted by their travels and the excitement of boarding, chose to retire early.

The following morning, Thursday, April 11, dawned so chilly and breezy that few passengers wanted to sit on deck. Instead, many toured the ship or enjoyed the public rooms. Third-class passengers had fewer public rooms to explore, but one group started up a skipping game outside on the aft well deck, and they were soon joined by others. In second class, the many children took over the enclosed promenade space at the aft end of C Deck, three decks below the Boat Deck, and it soon became their unofficial playground.

Later in the morning, passengers began gathering out on deck to look at the Irish coastline as they approached Queenstown. There, the liner anchored off Roche's Point while passengers and mail were tendered from shore.

At 1:30, the propellers began churning mud from the bottom of the harbor entrance as they started to turn, and the ship eased away from Queenstown for its westbound journey. After the pilot left the ship, she steamed along the south coast of Ireland for the rest of the afternoon. Finally, the land curved off to the north, gradually disappearing into the growing darkness. Many of the Irish emigrants who had just boarded knew this was probably the last time they would ever see their homeland.

The following two days — Friday and Saturday — were clear and sunny as the *Titanic* steamed toward New York, using the established southern route in order to avoid the

18

huge icebergs, icefields, and smaller bergs called "growlers" that sometimes floated down from the Arctic between January and August. All over the ship, crew and passengers settled into their new surroundings. In third class, passengers spent time in the open space below the forward well deck, while many of the men relaxed in the smoking room. The

skipping game that had begun en route to Queenstown was played again each day, often to the music of bagpipes that one passenger would bring out for the occasion. Some of the children discovered that empty cabins could be used as playrooms and wasted no time in taking them over.

First-class passengers enjoyed a wide variety of beautiful

Numerous ice warnings (opposite, left) were received in the *Titanic*'s Marconi Room by operators Jack Phillips (opposite, right) and assistant Harold Bride (opposite, middle). But not all of them were delivered to the bridge or shown to Captain Smith (far left). A message that arrived on Sunday, April 14, warning of field ice ahead, was given by Smith to J. Bruce Ismay (left), who later casually showed it to a passenger.

public rooms, including the Lounge, the Smoking Room, the Reading and Writing Room, the Verandah and Palm Courts, and the large Reception Room at the foot of the forward Grand Staircase. This elegant white-paneled room was a pleasant place to visit over coffee or tea after meals or to listen to the ship's musicians. On Saturday, April 13, Mrs. Elizabeth Lines of Paris chose a corner of the room to have a cup of coffee after luncheon. Captain Smith and Bruce Ismay entered as she was sitting there and took a seat only a few feet away.

"Well, we made a better run today than we did yesterday, " Ismay said to Smith. "We will make a better run tomorrow. Things are working smoothly, the machinery is bearing the test, the boilers are working well."

Smith nodded silently as Ismay spoke. Finally, Ismay brought his fist down on the arm of the settee and announced to Smith, "We will beat the *Olympic* and get in to New York on Tuesday!"

After breakfast the next morning, Sunday, April 14, Captain Smith presided over a Church of England service in the first-class Dining Saloon while the assistant purser, Reginald

At sea, smoking rooms were the domain of male passengers. The first-class smoking room (above, left), with its dark mahogany paneling inlaid with mother-of-pearl, its working fireplace and comfortable leather chairs, contrasted with the more austere surroundings of the third-class smoking room (above, right). Silverplated ashtrays and match holders (right) were also provided in the Dining Saloon and Reception Room for the use of first-class passengers.

Barker, conducted a service in second class. It was left to a second-class passenger, Father Thomas Byles, to hold a Catholic mass in the lounge for his fellow travelers before heading down to third class with another priest to say mass there.

Meanwhile, in the Marconi Room on the Boat Deck, the two operators, twenty-five-year-old Jack Phillips and twenty-one-year-old Harold Bride, did not have the luxury of taking Sunday off. They were working frantically to get caught up on a huge volume of messages. Sending personal wireless messages was a relatively new development, and many passengers were taking advantage of this latest mode of communication.

By this time, the *Titanic* had received several ice warnings from other ships. In the early afternoon, while on the bridge, Captain Smith showed Second Officer Lightoller one recently received from the Cunard liner *Caronia* reporting icebergs, growlers, and field ice ahead. After assessing the location of the sightings, Lightoller was relieved that they would not be reaching the ice-infested area during his watch from six to ten that evening. He estimated they would arrive there at about eleven.

At 1:40 P.M., another warning came in, this time from the White Star liner *Baltic*. It, too, reported ice, gave the location, and ended by saying that the *Deutschland*, a German tanker, was low on coal and wished to be reported to other steamers, hoping for a tow. Rather than posting the message

for his officers to see, Smith took it with him as he strolled aft on A Deck. There he encountered Bruce Ismay speaking with George and Eleanor Widener. Mr. Widener's father had the largest fortune in Philadelphia and was a director of the White Star Line's parent company, the International Mercantile Marine. Ismay would later claim that Smith handed him the telegram without saying a word. Yet a short time later, Ismay managed to tell another couple, Marian Thayer and her husband John B. Thayer, a vice-president of the Pennsylvania Railroad, that they would reach the ice around nine o'clock — something he would likely not have known unless Smith had told him.

Captain Smith was concerned enough about the ice that he ordered a maneuver to take the *Titanic* south of the normal route. It is unlikely he discussed his decision with Bruce Ismay. Normally, when sailing west during the spring, ships steamed southwest until they reached latitude 42° N, longitude 47° W — a location known as "the corner." By that point, commanders could feel that they were safely south of any ice, and they could then turn their ships due west to New York. The *Titanic* reached this position at 5:00 P.M., but Smith ordered that the change in course not be made until 5:45, causing the *Titanic* to steam an additional sixteen miles to the southwest before turning. Third Officer Herbert Pitman calculated that this put them ten miles south of the normal shipping route.

R.M.S. "TITANIC."
APRIL 14, 1912.

HORS D'ŒUVRE VARIÉS
OYSTERS

CONSOMMÉ OLGA   CREAM OF BARLEY
SALMON, MOUSSELINE SAUCE, CUCUMBER

FILET MIGNONS LILI
SAUTÉ OF CHICKEN, LYONNAISE
VEGETABLE MARROW FARCIE

LAMB, MINT SAUCE
ROAST DUCKLING, APPLE SAUCE
SIRLOIN OF BEEF, CHATEAU POTATOES

GREEN PEAS   CREAMED CARROTS
BOILED RICE
PARMENTIER & BOILED NEW POTATOES

PUNCH ROMAINE

ROAST SQUAB & CRESS
COLD ASPARAGUS VINAIGRETTE
PÂTÉ DE FOIE GRAS
CELERY

WALDORF PUDDING
PEACHES IN CHARTREUSE JELLY
CHOCOLATE & VANILLA ÉCLAIRS
FRENCH ICE CREAM

On the last evening at sea, George and Eleanor Widener (far left) hosted a dinner party, attended by Captain Smith, in the à la carte restaurant. Passengers eating in the Dining Saloon (opposite) made selections from the menu at left. (Below) This illustration evokes the spirit of elegant dining in 1912.

That evening, the dinner in first class was exceptionally elegant and the food seemed superior to the fare at any previous meal, with such elite items as filet mignon and roast squab. Many of the passengers dressed even more splendidly than usual for the occasion. Elmer Taylor, a manufacturer of paper cups, would later write that it seemed as if the women had brought out their finest gowns and best jewelry.

Captain Smith was not at his usual table in the first-class Dining Saloon that evening. Instead, he'd been invited to be a guest of the Wideners, along with Major Archibald Butt (President Taft's military aide) and two socially prominent Philadelphia couples, the William E. Carters and the John B. Thayers. They were dining in the à la carte restaurant on the aft end of B Deck. Although some passengers later claimed to have seen Smith there after nine, he had apparently left the group by that time, since Second Officer Lightoller later testified that the captain had appeared on

the bridge at 8:55. Smith had earlier estimated the ship would reach the ice at 9:00, and now he was making an appearance to see whether his prediction was correct. He and Lightoller talked about the possibility for the next twenty-five minutes, Smith indicating that if the cold, clear night became at all hazy they would have to slow down. "If in the slightest degree doubtful," the captain said in parting, "let me know." With that, he left the bridge at what was undoubtedly the most crucial point in the voyage.

After dinner, many passengers began settling in for the evening. In first class, some remained in the Reception Room to listen to the string orchestra while others drifted off to bed. The smoking rooms in each class were popular, and in steerage, a party that had started that afternoon in two of the public rooms now resumed, with music provided by the passengers themselves.

Shortly after 9:30, Wireless Operator Jack Phillips was in communication with Cape Race, Newfoundland, when a smaller steamer, the *Mesaba*, radioed the *Titanic*: "Ice report. In latitude 42° N to 41°25´ N, longitude 49° W to 50°30´ W.

(Far left) Built to make the *Titanic* "practically unsinkable," the massive double-cylinder watertight doors throughout the ship were designed to close quickly and immediately in an emergency by means of a powerful electromagnet — controlled from the bridge with a simple flick of an electric switch. A ladder or escape hatch provided an exit for the crewmen still working inside the sealed-off areas. First Officer William Murdoch (left) gave the initial order to close the doors.

Saw much heavy pack ice and great number large icebergs, also field ice. Weather good, clear." The *Mesaba*'s operator, Stanley Adams, knew that navigational messages took precedence over those sent by passengers, and waited to hear that this one, which described a huge field of ice into which the *Titanic* was steaming, had been reported to the bridge. Phillips only replied, "Received, thanks," and resumed his work with Cape Race.

At 10:38 P.M., the *Californian*, a cargo ship of the Leyland Line, suddenly interrupted with the warning, "We are stopped and surrounded by ice." The smaller ship was so near that her radio signals burst in on Phillips as if at full volume. "Shut up! Shut up!" he replied angrily. "I am busy. I am working Cape Race." Like the *Mesaba* message, this warning never reached the *Titanic*'s bridge. Instead, Phillips continued sending personal messages from passengers who were making hotel reservations in New York and advising loved ones of their impending arrival.

An hour later, the *Titanic* was still steaming at twenty-two and one-half knots, her full speed. First Officer William Murdoch was alone in command on the bridge. In the wheelhouse, Sixth Officer James Moody stood beside Quartermaster Robert Hichens, who was at the ship's wheel. Moody had only about twenty minutes left before his watch was finished and was probably looking forward to berthing down in his "cupboard-sized" cabin before his next watch at 4:00 A.M. Second Officer Lightoller had ordered the heat turned on in the officers' quarters and Moody was no doubt anticipating warming up before going on duty again.

Suddenly, the quiet night was interrupted by three strikes of the crow's nest bell, followed by the ringing of the telephone connecting the bridge to the lookouts. As Moody picked it up, he heard Lookout Frederick Fleet asking whether anyone was there.

"Yes," he replied. "What do you see?"

"Iceberg right ahead!"

"Thank you," Moody said and replaced the receiver. "Iceberg right ahead!" he called to Murdoch, but the First Officer had already seen the berg and rushed over to the engine room telegraph where he signaled "Full Speed Astern," and then called out "Hard a'starboard" to Hichens, who quickly swung the wheel hard over to port. (The "starboard" order still remained from the early days of sailing when putting the helm to starboard resulted in the ship turning to port.)

In the crow's nest, Frederick Fleet and Reginald Lee continued to watch the dark mass loom ahead of them. As they braced themselves, the nose of the ship began to turn to port. At first it appeared as though the ship might clear the iceberg, but there came from below a strange, scraping noise, and as the berg passed along the starboard bow, chunks

of ice began falling onto the forecastle and the well deck.

Meanwhile, far below, the iceberg was rupturing the hull of the ship. The first four watertight compartments were cargo areas, but the fifth was boiler room No. 6, where men were stoking the fires when a warning bell began ringing. High above, Murdoch had ordered the closing of the watertight doors, and as they began to shut, water came bursting in from the starboard side of the room about two feet above the floor plates. Men scrambled up the escape ladders and through the rapidly closing door.

In boiler room No. 5, the collision damage extended only into the forward coal bunker, and there only by a couple of feet. However, the first five compartments were hopelessly flooding, and this was one more than the ship could accommodate and still remain afloat.

Captain Smith appeared on the bridge soon after the collision, and Murdoch told him the bad news. Fourth Officer Joseph Boxhall had gone below to inspect the passenger areas and returned to report that no damage had been sustained there. Smith ordered him to send for the ship's carpenter to make an inspection, but Carpenter John Hutchinson was already on his way to the bridge to report that the ship was rapidly taking on water. A mail clerk came right behind Hutchinson, to report that the mail hold was filling fast. When Boxhall returned to say that he had personally seen the mail room flooding, Smith did not reply but turned and walked away.

Word of the collision was spreading quickly through the ship. In the bow, it was obvious that the vessel was taking on water. The quarters for the firemen were in the forepeak, and those who were lowest down began bringing their belongings to their mess room, higher up on C Deck, where they were teased by others who naively thought their own belongings were safe. Steerage men, whose cabins were also in the bow, found their rooms were beginning to flood. Many were soon heading aft with their luggage, but it's likely that some first carried them up to the third-class open space under the forward well deck.

In first-class cabin A-34, on the port side of the Promenade Deck, Dr. Washington Dodge, the tax assessor for the city of San Francisco, ventured out on deck, where he overheard other passengers talking about the collision being caused by ice. Walking to the forward end of the superstructure, he could look down onto the well deck, where ice lay strewn along the starboard rail. Steerage passengers were playfully kicking it about.

When the collision jolted Bruce Ismay awake, he thought the liner might have dropped a propeller blade, so he threw an overcoat over his pajamas and rushed up to the bridge. There, he asked Captain Smith what had happened.

"We have struck ice," Smith explained.

"Do you think the ship is seriously damaged?" Ismay asked.

"I am afraid she is."

Within half an hour, Captain Smith, Chief Officer Henry Wilde, Fourth Officer Boxhall, and Harland and Wolff managing director Thomas Andrews had all been below to inspect the flooding. As Andrews went past on the Grand Staircase, one passenger noticed a look of "terror" on his face. One of the *Titanic*'s designers, Andrews knew sooner than anyone else that the vessel was doomed. Not long after midnight, Captain Smith, now aware of the fate of his ship, gave the order to prepare the lifeboats.

Stewards began rousing the passengers throughout the *Titanic*. In second and third class, where there were fewer stewards per passenger, they pounded on doors and called out loudly for everyone to throw on their lifebelts and go on deck. In first class, most people were notified by a polite knock on the door. Henry Sleeper Harper, of the New York publishing family, was suffering from tonsilitis, but he had seen the iceberg pass his porthole and knew the collision must have been serious. Dr. William O'Loughlin confirmed the catastrophe when he stuck his head through Harper's doorway and said, "They tell me the trunks are floating around in the hold. You may as well go on deck." Harper and his wife slowly headed for the Boat Deck topside, where they sat down in the gymnasium.

At the foot of the Grand Staircase, on D Deck, where only the day before she had overheard Bruce Ismay boasting to Captain Smith about speeding to New York, Elizabeth Lines and her daughter encountered their bedroom steward. Minutes before, he had ordered them back to bed, but now he apparently knew the seriousness of the situation.

"You are going up on deck?" Mrs. Lines asked upon seeing him.

"No," he replied, and bade them goodbye.

Just before midnight, Assistant Wireless Operator Harold Bride woke up and stepped into the Marconi Room. There, Phillips explained that they had apparently struck something and might have to return to Harland and Wolff for repairs. A few minutes later, as Bride was urging Phillips to go to bed, Captain Smith appeared at the door.

"We've struck an iceberg and I'm having an inspection made to tell what it has done to us," he explained. "You had

(Below) A crewman aboard the *Olympic* conducts boat drill in the aftermath of the *Titanic* sinking. The *Titanic's* lifejackets, like these, were canvas vests filled with cork blocks. Ironically, while the gear kept many people from drowning, it afforded no protection from the freezing water that claimed most of the victims.

Captain Smith personally ordered the *Titanic*'s Marconi operators to send a distress signal, as shown in the dramatic illustration below. The brief yet urgent message (inset), taken down by the wireless operator on the *Baltic*, says simply "Sinking. Wants immediate assistance." (Opposite) A 1912 magazine illustration offers an idealized depiction of the scene on the Boat Deck during the loading of the lifeboats.

better get ready to send out a call for assistance, but don't send it until I tell you." When he returned ten minutes later, he handed them a sheet of paper with the ship's calculated position. "Send the call for assistance," he ordered.

"What call should I send?" Phillips asked.

"The regulation international call for help. Just that," Smith replied, and then left.

Phillips sat down at the key and tapped out the distress signal, "CQD," followed by the *Titanic*'s call letters, "MGY," half a dozen times. Meanwhile, he and Bride calmly joked about the situation.

Out on the Boat Deck, the mood was entirely different. People had begun to gather in the moonless night, shivering in the frigid air. First Officer Murdoch, fully aware of the danger they were now facing, did not hesitate to start loading and lowering the boats. On the starboard side of the ship, the boats were odd numbered, with boat No. 1 being the farthest forward. Boats 1 to 7 were in the first-class area, with a gap of nearly two hundred feet before boats 9 through 15, which were in second class. Murdoch began filling boat No. 7, but the passengers were reluctant to come forward and leave what they perceived to be the comfort and safety of an unsinkable ship. With so few passengers waiting to get in, he allowed both men and women to enter, gradually filling it with just over two dozen passengers and three crewmen. It was less than half full when he ordered it lowered and moved on to boat No. 5.

Bruce Ismay was near this lifeboat, instructing Third Officer Pitman to load it with women and children. "I await the commander's orders," Pitman replied abruptly, unaware that he was speaking to the

managing director of the White Star Line. Ismay then turned to a wealthy New York couple, the Richard L. Beckwiths, and urged them to get in. Mrs. Beckwith asked if everyone in their party could enter, and he replied, "Of course, Madam, every one of you." The Beckwiths, their daughter Helen Newsom, the Edwin Kimballs of Boston, and Helen's fiancé Karl Behr all stepped aboard.

"Are there any more women before this boat goes?" Ismay called out to the crowd. One came forward.

"Come along, jump in," he ordered.

"I am only a stewardess," the woman replied.

"Never mind," Ismay told her. "You are a woman. Take your place."

As the boat was being lowered, Ismay stood beside Fifth Officer Harold Lowe. Swinging his arm in huge circles, Ismay cried out with great excitement, "Lower away, lower away, lower away, lower away!" But Lowe had no idea who Ismay was, and instead of following orders, he exploded at the overwrought man. "Do you want me to lower away quickly? You will have me drown the whole lot of them!" Ismay said nothing, but turned and walked forward to boat No. 3. Nearby, Washington Dodge watched boat No. 5 descend, overwhelmed with wondering whether he'd done the right thing by sending his wife and small son out onto the open sea in the small craft.

On the port side, things were moving more slowly. Chief

(Left) Mrs. Isidor Straus would not leave her husband of forty years and refused to enter a lifeboat on the sinking liner. (Opposite) As the *Titanic* gradually settled down at the bow, steam was vented from pipes along her funnels, and distress rockets were sent high into the sky.

Officer Wilde did not yet appreciate the seriousness of the situation, and when Second Officer Lightoller asked him whether they should swing out the boats, he said no. Not satisfied with the response, Lightoller sought out Captain Smith and repeated the question. Smith told him to proceed. Then, when it came time to load the first boat, Wilde, apparently still unaware of the ship's condition, refused to allow Lightoller to put anyone in. Once again, Lightoller went to the captain, who again agreed with the second officer.

While these first boats were being loaded, steam from the boilers that would normally have driven the *Titanic's* engines was being vented from pipes running up the funnels. It made such a deafening roar that it was nearly impossible for people to hear one another. Then, suddenly, the noise stopped, leaving a silence that was soon broken by what sounded to the passengers and crew like music. The ship's musicians had been positioned on the port side of the Boat Deck, and they were playing ragtime and other cheerful tunes to calm and encourage the passengers.

Once Wilde was convinced of the catastrophic nature of the situation, all the port-side lifeboats began to be loaded, starting with the ones at the forward end of the ship. Initially, the plan was to load them from the A-deck promenade, just below the Boat Deck, to which lifeboat No. 4 was lowered, but the windows at the forward end were closed, so no one could exit from that level. The next plan was to load

boats 6 and 8 first. Among the passengers at boat No. 8 were Ida Straus and her husband Isidor, a partner in New York's R.H. Macy department store, who were completing a European holiday. Mrs. Straus had one foot on the gunwale of the lifeboat when she had a change of heart. "We have been living together for many years," she said, returning to her husband's side. "Where you go, I go." When friends urged the elderly Mr. Straus to enter one of the boats, he replied, "I will not go before the other men." The couple later moved away and sat down on a pair of deck chairs.

Suddenly, a burst of light came from the forward end of the starboard Boat Deck, and a rocket climbed above the masts and rigging, bursting into colored balls of light in the sky. Mrs. Emily Ryerson turned to her husband Arthur and said, "They wouldn't send those rockets unless it was the last."

The rockets were being fired because a ship had appeared in the distance. Unable to raise it by wireless, the *Titanic* was now using rockets and a Morse lamp to get its attention. It seemed to be approaching, yet ultimately the lights drew away and disappeared. The Leyland liner *Californian*, which had earlier sent an ignored ice warning, would take the blame for being this mysterious vessel, as its officers had watched a steamer send up rockets during the night without responding. However, the identity of this mystery ship has never been fully proven and remains a strongly debated topic to this day.

The forward lifeboats continued to be sent away holding fewer people than they had the capacity to carry. On the port side, Lightoller was prompt in lowering the boats, but none of them was full. He was interpreting "women and children first" to mean "women and children only" and was refusing to allow any men, aside from a few crewmen at the oars, to enter the boats. On the starboard side, Murdoch was allowing men to take to the boats if there still was room.

By the time the aft boats were being loaded, more and more passengers had found their way to the Boat Deck. For people from third class, this was often difficult. They did not normally have access to this deck, and finding their way through unfamiliar areas of the huge ship in order to reach the top deck was proving difficult. In many cases, doors remained locked, or their way was barred by crewmen who were allowing only women and children to pass. Many

As she closed the door of her cabin, first-class passenger Edith Rosenbaum (left) told a steward to be sure to check her luggage through to New York. John Jacob Astor (far right) tossed his gloves to his young wife Madeleine (right) as she was lowered in lifeboat No. 4.

steerage passengers simply headed to the aft well deck, where they waited to be told what to do.

Those who did reach the boats found that the decks were now crowded, and as a result, on the starboard side fewer men were being allowed to escape. At the same time, some of the women were still reluctant to go out onto the open, freezing sea. When Edith Rosenbaum, a writer for the Paris offices of *Women's Wear Daily*, hesitated to enter boat No. 11, a crewman grabbed a musical toy pig she was clutching and threw it into the boat, hoping she would follow. With some help climbing over the railing, she did. As more women and children approached, however, the crew realized they could not take everyone and began denying entry to any adult.

Back on the port side, so many men were crowding the rail as boat No. 14 was being lowered that Fifth Officer Lowe, fearful that they might jump in, pulled out his revolver and fired it along the side of the ship to prevent anyone from doing so. By now, it was nearing 2:00 A.M. It had been over an hour since boat No. 4 had first been lowered to the A-deck promenade, and now Lightoller was preparing to fill it by placing deck chairs against the rail to act as steps so that women and children could enter through the large rectangular windows, which had since been opened. Madeleine Astor was passed through one of these by Colonel Archibald Gracie, a military historian from Washington, D.C. Second Officer Lightoller, standing in the boat, took her aboard.

Because she was pregnant, her husband leaned out one of the windows and asked if he could go with her to protect her. "No, sir," Lightoller replied. "No men are allowed in these boats until women are loaded first." After asking the number of the lifeboat, Astor tossed his gloves to his wife.

In addition to the sixteen wooden lifeboats, there were four shallow boats with collapsible canvas sides, labeled alphabetically. Collapsibles C and D were stored beneath the davits for boats 1 and 2, respectively, while A and B were on the roof of the officers' quarters just aft of the bridge. On the starboard side, the davits from boat No. 1 had been cranked back in and the falls attached to collapsible C. A group of men began scrambling into the boat ahead of the women and children, causing one of the officers to fire his pistol into the air, crying out, "Get out of this! Clear out of this!" The men were dragged out of the boat, and women and children were loaded in. Nevertheless, two first-class male passengers, William E. Carter and White Star managing director J. Bruce Ismay, scrambled into the boat. First Officer Murdoch made no objection to their getting on board, and the lifeboat was lowered to the water, its gunwales scraping along the ship's rivets as it descended.

Lightoller, still on the port side, was loading collapsible D and also had to use his gun to keep the men back. The crew linked arms to form a ring around the boat, through which only women and children could pass.

A short distance aft in the Marconi Room, the lights were growing dim. Throughout the sinking, the wireless operators had been in touch with a number of vessels, but none was close enough to arrive in time for a rescue. Only the Cunard liner *Carpathia* gave them any hope, but even she was nearly sixty miles away and would not arrive for several more hours. Finally, Captain Smith entered the room and said to Bride and Phillips, "Men, you have done your full duty. You can do no more. Abandon your cabin." The men did not move. "You look out for yourselves," he continued. "I release you." It was the last time Smith would enter the wireless room. In spite of Smith's command, Phillips continued to work at the key. Bride stepped into their sleeping quarters to pocket his spare money, and when he returned, he found a stoker had entered the Marconi Room and was removing the lifebelt Bride had put on Phillips. The junior operator grabbed the man, and Phillips leapt to his feet and swung at him until he collapsed to the floor. Hearing water pouring onto the bridge nearby, the two men left the stoker to his fate and ran from the room.

Forward on the Boat Deck, men were struggling to lower the remaining collapsibles from the roof of the officers' quarters. They swarmed around the boats and set oars against the bulkheads to slide them down. Both came crashing onto the deck, smashing some of the oars, and while A landed upright, B was upside down. The men began attach-

ing A to the falls of boat No. 1's davit when Captain Smith approached with a megaphone and shouted, "Well, boys, do your best for the women and children, and look out for yourselves."

Suddenly, the bow of the *Titanic* began to plunge, creating a huge wave that washed aft across the Boat Deck. People scrambled aboard collapsibles A and B as the two boats floated from the deck. Others began instinctively running aft, while still more poured out of the entrance to the first-class Grand Staircase. Some began jumping from the ship, and as the stern continued to rise, still more passengers slid back down the deck toward the dark, freezing waters. Others clung to anything they could, often each other. From deep inside the ship came a huge roaring noise as luggage, furniture, and anything else that wasn't fastened down began sliding. Then, as the bridge dipped under the surface of the ocean, the first funnel, just aft of the bridge, fell forward, crashing onto some of the swimmers. It washed collapsibles A and B away and plunged their occupants into the icy waters. But some managed to swim back to the collapsibles and cling to them like rafts.

When the ship neared a forty-five-degree incline, all the lights went out, leaving it in darkness as it began to break in two at a point between the third and fourth funnels. The tremendous weight of the engines in the stern, just aft of the rear expansion joint and the aft Grand Staircase, tore the ship in two and brought the stern crashing back down onto the

(Right) As the *Titanic*'s bow sank deeper, the ship suddenly broke in two, sending the aft end, crowded with passengers and crew, crashing back down onto the sea. For a few moments, those in the lifeboats thought that the stern might float on its own — but then it, too, upended and sank beneath the surface.

water. The forward half of the ship disappeared beneath the surface. The stern then rose up again until it was almost perpendicular to the water. There it remained motionless for what survivors estimated to be anywhere from thirty seconds to several minutes before it plunged straight down, slowly at first, but with increasing speed. At 2:20 A.M., it disappeared, and in its place rose the screams and cries of the hundreds of passengers and crew who had remained on board, and who were now freezing to death in the twenty-eight-degree water. For those in the lifeboats, the screams coming out of the darkness were sounds they would never forget.

The occupants of the lifeboats were so intimidated by the struggling throng of swimmers that lifeboats 4 and 14 were the only two to make any attempt to return for survivors, and they saved only a handful each. By 3:00 A.M, over fifteen hundred people were dead, and the remaining seven hundred and eleven waited in the boats on the open sea for dawn and rescue. The two would arrive together, when the *Carpathia* appeared at 4:00 A.M. and started recovering those in the lifeboats. By 8:30 A.M., the operation was over and the Cunard liner began the long voyage to New York. The entire world awaited its arrival.

Chapter Two *Diving to the Wreck*

In 1914, the magazine *Popular Mechanics* predicted that the children of some who went down in the *Titanic* might "live to look upon an actual picture of that great steamship resting on the ocean floor." The article went on to describe the latest developments in underwater photography, including a description of motion pictures that could already be taken under the surface of the ocean by using an "ingenious" four-foot sphere with a three-inch-thick plate-glass window at one end. The sphere could be lowered to a maximum depth of three hundred feet from a barge that had been appropriately named after science-fiction writer Jules Verne.

Just over seventy years later, the *Popular Mechanics* prediction came true. In 1985, the *Titanic* was discovered by a joint American-French team headed by Dr. Robert Ballard of the Woods Hole Oceanographic Institution, and the images they captured were seen not only by children of victims but even by some of the survivors themselves. In the nearly two decades since, the wreck has been explored by many more divers. Some went to salvage artifacts; others set out specifically to film the *Titanic*. Two of these photographic expeditions were led by filmmaker James Cameron: one in 1995 for his 1997 movie *Titanic*, and another in 2001. For this last mission, I joined him on August 14, 2001, in the harbor at St. John's, Newfoundland, as he was preparing to leave for the site of the wreck. Ken Marschall and I had been hired as historical advisors for this voyage — part of a small

corps of consultants, actors, and scientists who would contribute to Jim's new large-format three-dimensional documentary film about the *Titanic*. Ken, the renowned maritime artist who had created haunting paintings of the *Titanic* wreck for various books including Robert Ballard's *Discovery of the Titanic*, is also an expert on the sunken ship's structure and interiors. As historian of the U.S.-based Titanic Historical Society, I'd known many *Titanic* survivors personally, and the ship's history had become part of my daily work and life. But I never thought I'd have the opportunity to see the wreck myself.

Seagulls wheeled and cried in the close mid-August air as Jim, Ken, and I picked our way along the deck of the *Akademik Mstislav Keldysh*, the Russian research vessel that would become our home for the next several weeks. Jim was giving us a quick tour of the equipment we would be using, and we had to be careful to avoid the yards of electrical lines that had been installed around the ship for lights and cameras.

Intense and focused when directing his crew, Jim has the mind of an engineer and always appears to have planned and revised every detail of his projects personally. For this expedition, he had mentally coordinated everything that needed to be done and was continually refining his approach — even to the point of sending director John Bruno to find out whether there were any nearby icebergs that could be

(Below) The *Akademik Mstislav Keldysh*, with two deep-sea submersibles on board, arrives in the harbor at St. John's, Newfoundland. Over four hundred feet long, the Russian ship is one of the few research vessels equipped to handle the dive to the *Titanic* wreck, located two and a half miles beneath the surface of the North Atlantic.

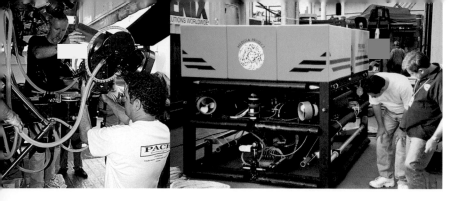

filmed. When Jim isn't concentrating solely on his work, however, he has a casual manner and is always ready for an animated conversation with those who share his interest in underwater exploration.

Early on in our tour, Jim showed us the controls of one of the 3-D high-definition cameras that would be used to film the exterior of the wreck. Launching into two of his favorite topics — technology and physics — he demonstrated how the camera's two lenses angled toward or away from each other, depending on the distance of the object that was being filmed. Though Jim has high standards and is known for being critical when things don't measure up to his expectations, he can also show great patience as he describes complex technical processes — especially in the context of his longstanding love, the *Titanic*.

Jim was particularly eager to tell us about the new Remotely Operated Vehicles (ROVs), nicknamed 'bots, that had been developed exclusively for this mission. It had taken a team — led by his brother Mike — three years to build robots small enough to enter and film parts of the ship that other, larger ROVs had been unable to reach. Designed to withstand deep-sea water pressure of 8,000 pounds per square inch, the 'bots also had unusually long fiber-optic tethers that would spool out from the ROVs themselves, allowing them to wander far from the MIR submersibles from which they would be operated. Later dubbed Elwood and Jake, after

the Blues Brothers, the ROVs would be the techno-stars of the expedition, along with an underwater chandelier lighting system, also custom-designed for this film. Jim has often said that the crucial thing about deep-sea photography is lighting — and this new system, called *Medusa*, would cast a moonlight glow over the wreck, creating a ghostly effect.

As we moved along the starboard side of the ship, Jim pointed out the submersibles, *MIR-1* and *MIR-2* — the vehicles that would take us down to the ocean floor. We would usually dive with Russian senior pilot Anatoly Sagalevitch and Evgeny "Genya" Cherniev, who had helped design and build the subs in the 1980s.

Jim was soon called away, so Ken and I kept wandering on our own. We passed the production office (a tiny room near the top of the gangway) and a laboratory that had been set aside for microbiology studies. This was the main residence of microbiologist Lori Johnston, who would be analyzing the wreck's "rusticles" — complex bacterial communities that grow on iron shipwrecks like icicles.

Throughout the voyage, all activities would be photographed — either in 3-D, by a video cameraman, or by several stationary "spy-cams" that had been mounted in a number of locations around the ship. As Jim would say, he wanted to "catch Sasquatch in the forest." (The spy-cams were so well hidden that I even bumped my head on one later in the expedition.) The camera count was especially

high because several films were being made at once. Though Jim's 3-D documentary took center stage, Jim's brother John David was overseeing a live Internet broadcast under the name EarthShip.tv — and the resident videographer aboard the *Keldysh*, Sergey Kudriashov, was creating documentaries for Russian television.

All the impressive technology and expertise on board would be taxed to the limit as Jim's pioneering effort took us to parts of the *Titanic* that had not been seen for almost ninety years. With space on the *Keldysh* for only thirty team members, Jim had to work with a much smaller film crew than he would have had on a movie set. And since the documentary would often be filmed in restrictive, undersea conditions, there would be few opportunities for retakes.

As sailing day approached, the weather was as fickle as it often is in Newfoundland. When the days weren't hot and muggy, they were drizzly, until at last the skies cleared. Hurricane season was approaching, but Jim could not afford months of further delay before starting the expedition — and the newly designed equipment could not have been ready sooner. In fact, as we sailed out of the harbor, well after dark on Friday, August 17, Elwood and Jake were still in California undergoing final checks and preparations. After about a week of filming the exterior of the wreck, we would come back to St. John's to pick up the 'bots for our first forays into the unknown regions of the ship's interior.

A crowd of well-wishers had gathered on the dock, some waving white handkerchiefs. They grew smaller and smaller as we pulled away from shore, then vanished completely into the night. Before we launched out into the open sea, I looked back one last time in the direction of Signal Hill, where the Italian inventor Guglielmo Marconi had received the first transatlantic wireless transmission in 1901, about a decade before the Marconi wireless room was installed on the *Titanic*. Then, like my companions on the *Keldysh*, I turned my thoughts to our destination, 36 hours away — 375 miles southeast of St. John's, and about 1,000 miles due east of Boston.

I began to understand, more than ever, the daunting nature of the task facing us some two and a half miles below the surface of the dark and cold Atlantic. I had to remind myself that this was not the first *Titanic* expedition, and it would surely not be the last. But no previous missions had unlocked the secrets of what lay inside the wreck. How much of the ship's elegant cabins and public rooms remained? Or was the interior simply a ruin shrouded in rust and silt? We all believed there could be many new treasures inside the *Titanic*, and there was a noticeable energy aboard the *Keldysh* because we knew the remains of the ship were about to be filmed in a more spectacular way than ever before.

On August 18, our first full day at sea, I awoke at seven and went down for breakfast just before eight, expecting to see a crowd of people enjoying their bacon and eggs before our 8:30 A.M. production meeting in the ship's outdated computer center, dubbed "Mission Control." To my surprise, the dining room was almost empty and the generous breakfast buffet had hardly been touched. Perhaps this was our last chance to sleep in, and the more experienced members of the team were wisely resting up for the long working days that lay ahead.

After breakfast, I went down to Mission Control, below the ship's waterline, where Jim also commented on the low turnout. But as the meeting went on, more people arrived and clustered around the light table. There were only a few chairs, so most leaned against the pole that supported the ceiling or rested against the ancient freestanding dot-matrix printers left over from Russia's Cold War days. Others stood in front of countertops cluttered with the video equipment Jim had brought on board at St. John's.

Whether we were at sea or in port, the production-meeting ritual happened every morning after breakfast. Jim usually conducted the meetings while director John Bruno filmed them. But there were times when Jim couldn't resist pointing out a better camera angle or taking over the direction completely.

On this particular morning, Jim talked about safety issues for the coming weeks, focusing especially on the rubber Zodiac boat. There was no reason, he said, for anyone to be on the water unless it was to support the MIR submersibles as they dived down to the wreck, operate rescue equipment, or do underwater photography. We were also told many times never to go out on the open decks without telling someone, especially in rough weather. All equipment had to be secured and not left lying around. If the weather took a turn for the worse, any loose gear could become a dangerous projectile. A stray pile of high-tech clutter could also show up on camera, making the documentary look too much like a movie about producing a film.

By this time, Jim had realized that he needed an A.D. — an assistant director. For the time being, he chose Rich Robles, a staff member who would wear a number of hats during the expedition. His duties, Jim said, were to keep track of everything and everyone at once, always staying at Jim's side in case he needed something. It also sometimes meant being the fall guy — and a loud one at that. "It means a lot of pressure," said Jim. "Everybody hates you. They can either hate me or you, so ... " We all knew what that meant.

Once the production meetings were over, some team members did not return to Mission Control until the next day, but Ken and I — and Jim's creative producer and chief editor, Ed Marsh — spent many hours there. In fact, we rarely saw Ed outside Mission Control. His presence was

most often felt in other parts of the ship over the radio as a disembodied voice — for which he earned the name "Oz." But his primary role, here among the unused, outdated computers, was to digitize the dive footage, log the tapes, and coordinate the projection of new video footage. The 3-D shots from the wreck were screened in the lounge from a projector fed by the tapes in Mission Control, many decks below.

In our role as historians, Ken and I were put to work with Lewis Abernathy — who'd played one of the sub crew in the 1997 movie — drafting visual navigational aids to help the divers when they went down to the *Titanic*. I iden-

tified known occupants of various first-class cabins and labeled them on the deck plans while Ken created drawings of each side of the bow and an overhead view. Then Lewis overlaid a grid pattern on each of the drawings.

These diagrams were sent down with the two MIR subs and also given to the crew on the *MT Eas*, our smaller companion vessel — a Dynamic Positioning ship, which held the *Medusa* lighting system in place. By referring to the individual grids, all parties could tell one another where they were on the *Titanic* or where they were supposed to go, even if they were not familiar with any of the decks or features themselves.

When we arrived at the site of the wreck on the afternoon of August 19, we were welcomed by a whale, which the Russians sighted from the port bridge wing. It vanished into the calm ocean soon afterward, and the only sea life left to break the capacious silence were birds skimming close to the water and occasionally resting on the surface. As our ship drifted, one of these seabirds flew into the cabin of Bill Paxton, who'd played the explorer Brock Lovett in the 1997 *Titanic* movie and was on this trip to narrate his personal reactions. Before long, the bird had flown back out to the quiet sea, and we were left to drift above the wreck and wait for diving day.

Twelve dives were planned. The first had been scheduled for August 20, but camera problems postponed the mission. Though Bill was a veteran of many action films, he admitted he was a bit nervous about going down two and a half miles to the bottom of the ocean — and the delay didn't help. As a husband and father, he wondered whether he should even be diving. "It's one of those moments," he said, "when you need to make sure your will is in order and your insurance is paid up."

But there was no going back now, and on the morning of August 21, the Russians and the American camera team crowded into the MIR lab for the MIR meeting, always held on dive days right before the production meeting. The lab was a small workshop just inboard from where the *MIR-1* and *MIR-2* subs were lashed to the deck, and most of the space in the room was taken up by a large work table. So every MIR meeting was crowded, with people jammed up beside the cabinets along the walls or leaning against the sink beside one of the doors. Anatoly Sagalevitch, the senior MIR pilot, announced that a dive would take place that day, since the weather was suitable. John Bruno and Bill would dive in *MIR-2*, which always did the lighting for the 3-D camera on *MIR-1*. Jim would dive in *MIR-1* with Vince Pace, and he would operate the camera that Vince had built. Anatoly would pilot *MIR-1* and Genya Cherniev would fly *MIR-2*.

Jim's sub was always launched first. A small crowd usually assembled on deck and watched from above as Jim and a second diver would enter, followed by either Anatoly or Genya. The filming of the launch would be directed by John Bruno unless he himself was diving, and John would be put in charge of all filming on board the *Keldysh* until Jim returned. Once *MIR-1* resurfaced, however, and Jim had climbed out, he would be right behind the cameras again, directing the recovery of *MIR-2*.

All divers signed a log book kept by the Russians before donning their blue dive suits. Then their outfit was issued under the watchful eye of Lydia, one of the Russian crew, whose stern countenance told you not to question and never to contradict. It was Lydia who once warned Bill not to whistle on the ship. According to an old mariner's superstition, whistling summoned the wind.

At about mid-morning, as the sun broke through the overcast sky, Jim climbed up the side of *MIR-1*. "See you in the sunshine," he grinned before he disappeared down the hatch.

"This is the moment of truth," Bill said as he climbed down into *MIR-2*.

As we watched, safe on deck, *MIR-1* was swung out into the ocean, still attached by an enormously thick cable to a crane leaning out over the side. At the same time, the sub was clamped between two gigantic mechanical arms, designed to turn it and also to keep it from pivoting left or right. Then a tightly choreographed launching ritual began. A motorboat called the *Koresh* had been lowered into the water before the MIRs left the deck, with its pilot Lev, a young Russian known as The Rope Handler, and one of the "cowboys" on board. The Zodiac was launched from the starboard side of the *Keldysh* with its own pilot Guyenna and another cowboy. The Zodiac picked up the first cowboy from the *Koresh*, then motored right up to *MIR-1*. When it arrived at the side of the sub, one of the cowboys performed the daredevil act of jumping from the Zodiac to the MIR and unhooking the cable that held the MIR to the crane.

Then the *Koresh* towed the sub away from the *Keldysh*, the cowboy standing on top of the MIR like a rodeo performer on the back of a horse. When the MIR was far enough away, the cowboy unhooked the tow line from the

(Below) In a series of tightly choreographed maneuvers, the *MIR-1* is readied for its first dive. From the Zodiac at right, one of the "cowboys" prepares to jump onto the back of the submersible to detach the crane cable. Once the motorboat *Koresh*, at left, tows the *MIR-1* safely away from the *Keldysh*, the submersible will begin its descent. (Opposite, left) Inside *MIR-2*, pilot Genya Cherniev seals the hatch prior to launch. (Opposite, right) Bill Paxton, right, gets his first glimpse of the *Titanic* wreck.

sub, then jumped back into the Zodiac, which sped away while the tow line was hauled aboard the *Koresh*. Now *MIR-1* was free to head down to the ocean floor.

Over in *MIR-2*, Genya was turning the locking mechanism on the white hatch door to shut it tight against the ocean. He had a bristly, light brown mustache, a shy countenance, and a gaze that was quick but calm and concentrated. Once Genya was settled, *MIR-2* was launched and began to move through the turquoise upper-ocean waters. Bill looked out a porthole and saw a diver taking a picture of the sub with an underwater camera. As the diver swam up toward the golden light shining through the ocean's surface, Bill knew that would be his last sight of "home" for many hours.

"It's amazing how fast it goes dark," Bill said, as the submersible sank away from the sunlit waters.

While the men worked and talked, *MIR-2* kept forging a path down through the silent darkness — 1,000 feet, 2,000 feet — a journey that would take roughly two and a half hours.

Then, suddenly, they were at the very bottom of the ocean. Stretching out before them was a nearly featureless floor of grayish silt, marked only by a lone starfish and skid tracks from previous sub dives. "It's like the dark side of the moon," Bill remarked as he looked out his porthole.

Genya turned on the SIMRAD Mesotech acoustic imaging sonar and scanned the area in front of the MIR, look-ing for his target — the bow of the *Titanic*. In minutes, something appeared on the monitor: a frieze of cascading bronze rusticles, topped by intact railings — the bow of the wreck, still majestic in *MIR-2*'s lights. On the starboard side, they saw the bow anchor still in position, glowing blue-green and covered with small waterfalls of rust. All around them, there was what looked like a continual light snowstorm — backscatter from the MIR's lights as their beams reflected off particles floating in the water. It was sea snow, an underwater galaxy that would surround them as they explored the wreck.

Like a curious beetle, the orange and white body of *MIR-2* edged up closer to the hull. Then the sub headed up and over the nose of the ship, clearing the anchor crane and moving above the deck of the forecastle, where the *Titanic*'s gigantic anchor chains stretched out in parallel like abandoned railway tracks disappearing into a desert of silt and snow.

"Mast door," said Genya seconds later as *MIR-2* floated up along the fallen mast. Draped with rusticles that looked like Spanish moss on a southern cypress, the huge column still showed its open doorway, where crewmen exited after climbing up inside the mast to the crow's nest. Bill later described the experience of drifting over the ruins on deck as ethereal — as if he were a ghost of the *Titanic* himself. But it was also exciting work, exploring the *Titanic* with new technologies and "touching the legend" of this magnificent ship.

Finally, there was the ruined bridge itself, where the telemotor that once held the ship's wheel still stood, its bronze column gleaming in the sub's lights.

"Quite a ride!" said Bill as he emerged from the sub, back on the ocean's surface. Later, he admitted that the experience not only was vivid but also chilled him to the bone, and at one point he felt he had to leave. "I felt like we were disturbing her," he said. "I guess you feel like she's sleeping."

Jim was amazed at the shots he'd captured. He told us he'd taken more good footage in the first hour of this trip than he had during the entire month he'd spent filming in 1995.

On August 30, we arrived back in St. John's to pick up the breadbox-sized ROVs, the ROV team, and their forty shipping cases' worth of gear. As we entered the harbor, a dramatic sunset greeted our return, and the weather had turned noticeably cooler. Fall was approaching, with its higher winds and hurricane warnings, so we had little time to lose.

"The 'bots are finally going to *Titanic*," Jim said as preparations were made for the first dive using the ROVs. "Three years in the making." Now, at the bottom of the ocean, they would face their greatest test.

On September 5, back at the wreck, ROV pilot Jeff Ledda brought Jake, the blue ROV, out of his garage on *MIR-2* and

landed him on the deck of the *Titanic*; Jim piloted green Elwood, who emerged from *MIR-1* to join his companion.

Jeff then sent Jake down the opening in the ship that had once held the forward Grand Staircase. A beautiful wrought-iron-and-glass dome originally stood over an oak-paneled staircase there, but now it was an enormous gaping hole that allowed easy entry into the ship's interior.

"Okay, we're going to come out and meet you in the center of the Grand Staircase," *MIR-2* radioed to Jim as Jake headed that way.

"Tell them to move ahead slowly," said Jim.

"Moving ahead slow."

"Okay, we're at the D-deck landing in the Reception Room at the bottom of the stairs," said Jim. "The Dining Saloon is just around the corner. Out."

"So what are your instructions?" asked one of the men in *MIR-2*.

"Move forward to that door frame," said Jim in his measured, concentrated way.

"Copy that."

"Come up a bit. You're too close to the bottom."

Jake and Elwood successfully sent back images to the monitors in their MIRs, but with their thirty-five-watt spotlights and fifteen-watt floodlights, they could not fully illuminate the rooms. Jim later said it was like trying to light a football field with a flashlight.

Before long, Jake and Elwood had stirred up enough silt within the wreck that visibility was lost, and the 'bots were withdrawn.

Back on the surface, the ROV team stayed up late, trying to solve the silting-out problem. In the end, they decided that Jim and Jeff needed to change their flying techniques — they would have to cruise the 'bots farther apart, cut out the fast turns, and keep them higher above the silt-covered floors.

Two days later, on the second 'bot dive, Jim and Jeff sent Elwood and Jake back down to D Deck, to explore the Dining Saloon, the Reception Room, and the staterooms forward of the Grand Staircase.

Moving aft, Elwood and Jake entered the cavernous first-class Dining Saloon, where rusting, cast-iron bases of tables rose from the silt and debris on the floor. Then Jim and Eric Schmitz in *MIR-1* and Jeff and Bill in *MIR-2* came upon a completely unexpected scene — two ornate leaded-glass windows, five feet tall, their brass handles still in place and the wood paneling on either side in surprisingly good condition. A short distance away, the floor sloped off and the ceiling angled down even more sharply toward it. This is where the ship had broken in two.

As the lights from Jake and Elwood shone amber off the windows, the leaded-glass patterns were still dramatically clear.

(Opposite, left) Bill Paxton gives Jake an encouraging pat before the ROV undergoes pre-dive testing in the small pool at right. (Opposite, right) With Elwood in the foreground, the two 'bots explore the port Boat Deck. An electric winch used for lifting lifeboats is visible just behind Elwood. (Below) Inside the *Titanic*, looking toward the stairwell on A Deck. A crystal-beaded light fixture hangs by its wire.

"Look at that. Still intact!" exclaimed Bill. "It's all there. Not broken."

"Unbelievable," said Jim. "Who would have thought that would still be there!"

Retracing their route, Jake and Elwood moved back through the Reception Room, where more intact leaded-glass windows appeared. Here, much of the carved paneling still covered the walls, and floor-to-ceiling columns still stood in place — although a large lavender-colored worm-like creature could be seen in the woodwork.

The 'bots moved on, past the remains of the bronze grilled doors that graced the starboard first-class entrance vestibule. Then, inside the outer gangway door, their lights shone on another first: elegant floor-to-ceiling wrought-iron gates with brass handles, almost as whole as they'd been when passengers had entered the ship at Cherbourg. No photographs of these gates were known to exist, from either the *Olympic* or the *Titanic* — until this moment.

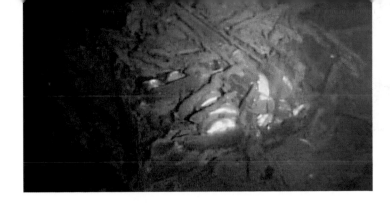

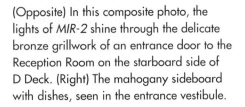

(Opposite) In this composite photo, the lights of *MIR-2* shine through the delicate bronze grillwork of an entrance door to the Reception Room on the starboard side of D Deck. (Right) The mahogany sideboard with dishes, seen in the entrance vestibule.

Near these large gangway gates, a mahogany sideboard lay face down, its White Star china visible through the back, where the wood had rotted away. Amazingly, the dishes had made it all the way down to the bottom of the ocean — unbroken and still neatly stacked!

Because Jake's and Elwood's tethers were so long, the 'bots kept going farther from their subs, heading for the passenger staterooms, where they were guided gently through five of them. Watching on the monitor in *MIR-2*, Bill noticed that, unlike the heavy mahogany Reception Room paneling, the thinner pine walls between the cabins were almost entirely gone. In the distance, he could make out poles rising from the silt, debris, and fallen rusticles. As the camera moved closer, he realized they were bedposts. And lying on top of many of the beds were large, rectangular boxes — fallen upper bunks that had once folded up against the now-missing walls.

As Jake and Elwood scanned the floors, collapsed washstands — pulled over by the heavy porcelain basins as their wooden frames decayed — appeared on the monitors in the two MIRs. Then, to everyone's surprise, there loomed ahead of the ROVs one washstand still upright, its mirror intact. On the remains of a wooden shelf on one side of the mirror, an upright carafe appeared, with a water glass standing on the shelf below — as if still waiting for the room's occupant to take a drink.

As the two ROVs moved back to the Reception Room, *MIR-1*'s Eric Schmitz looked down at the laptop computer that was monitoring Elwood's performance. A warning light had come on. The 'bot's battery, normally between fifteen and sixteen volts, had dropped to twelve. Eric notified Jim instantly, but even as he spoke, the voltage dropped again, to eleven. Schmitz knew Elwood was in trouble.

In *MIR-1*, four decks above, Jim couldn't see Elwood for himself, so he radioed Jeff to fly Jake over to take a look: "Guys, get a visual on us because we just lost power."

It was already too late. The voltage in Elwood's battery dropped to seven and a half and the computer monitor went dead as the green ROV stopped sending back signals.

"Headed for the ceiling, Jim. Headed for the ceiling."

"We're dead in the water! We have a low battery."

Jim put his hands over his eyes and his head dropped forward.

In *MIR-2*, Jeff and Bill could see that Elwood had risen upward as small bubbles erupted from its back — created by an apparent chemical reaction. Gradually, the ROV settled on the ceiling in the starboard D-deck entrance vestibule, the bubbles indicating that his battery had exploded.

A new dimension had suddenly been added to the mission. We had a new wreck on our hands. And the only piece of equipment that could enter the ship to rescue Elwood was his companion, Jake.

In addition to capturing the *Titanic*'s haunting interiors, James Cameron's tiny ROVs added some new paragraphs to the ever-unfolding story of the legendary liner. In particular, they highlighted previously unknown differences between the *Olympic* and the *Titanic*. The most surprising of these was the number of additional columns supporting the ceiling in the *Titanic*'s Reception Room. Other, smaller changes included the design of the elevators' grillwork doors and the ceiling lights in the elevator lobby.

The expedition also revealed unknown similarities between the two ships. Identical matches to *Olympic* photos were seen in the patterns of the leaded-glass windows in the Reception Room and Dining Saloon, in the range of light fixtures used in the different public rooms and in the design of the double doors that led from the D-deck entrance vestibule. In the past, information about the *Olympic* was used to imagine the *Titanic*. Where no photographs exist of areas of either ship, we can now study the *Titanic* wreck to imagine the *Olympic*.

(Left) The massive prow of the *Titanic*, still intact after ninety years on the ocean bottom, is the most recognizable feature of the now-famous wreck. (Inset) Period postcards of the White Star liner, such as this one by Raphael Tuck & Sons, Art Publishers to Their Majesties the King and Queen, were available on board the *Titanic* and in shops

The Foc's'le and Mast

The *Titanic*'s forecastle — or foc's'le, as the crew called it — was virtually identical to that of her sister ship, the *Olympic,* shown in the photograph at left. (Below) *MIR-2*'s lights illuminate the capstans and windlasses that secured ropes and anchor chains.

Lookout Frederick Fleet (bottom inset, left) and his mates would have climbed up a ladder inside the mast to reach the crow's nest that towered more than ninety feet above the ocean (bottom inset, right). The fallen mast now lies across the well deck (inset, top). (Above) The doorway of the crow's nest, with its hand grips intact. Although the bracket that held the warning bell is still fitted above, the bell itself was found in the debris field in 1987.

Lookout Frederick Fleet

"Is there any more likes to have a go at me?" asked a defiant Frederick Fleet after giving evidence at the British Inquiry into the *Titanic's* loss. As the lookout who first sighted the iceberg, he was questioned closely about his actions that night. Disagreeing with fellow lookout Reginald Lee, who testified that there had been a thick haze on the horizon, Fleet stated that the haze was so slight as to be "nothing to talk about." Young Fleet had been raised in one of England's famed Dr. Barnardo orphanages and was sent to sea at the age of twelve. A deckhand at sixteen, he worked his way up to lookout on the *Titanic* nine years later. After his escape from the stricken *Titanic* in lifeboat No. 6, Fleet worked on ships for the next twenty-four years, always for meager wages. In his old age, he sold newspapers on a street corner in Southampton. In 1965, despondent over his wife's recent death, he took his own life.

The bridge was at the top and forward end of the ship's superstructure (opposite, top left). A now-famous photograph of the interior of the *Olympic*'s bridge (opposite, top right), taken by Jesuit student Francis Browne, who would later sail on the *Titanic* from Southampton to Queenstown. All that remains of the area today is the solitary telemotor (opposite,

bottom). It was at this instrument that Quartermaster Robert Hichens quickly swung the wheel hard over to port in a desperate bid to steer the *Titanic* clear of the looming iceberg. Captain Smith (left) had a private bathroom adjacent to his quarters on the Boat Deck. The marble sink still remains (bottom right), as do the bathtub (top right) and the many pipes that provided either hot and cold fresh water or hot and cold seawater. (Insets) A similar sink and bathtub.

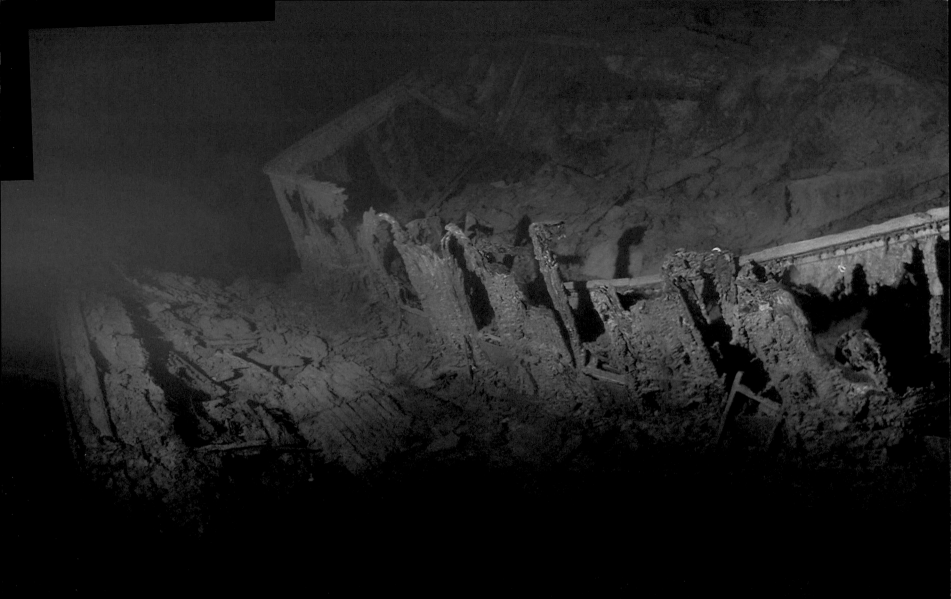

The Gymnasium

Once one of the *Titanic's* most popular public rooms, the gymnasium has deteriorated greatly since the ship's discovery in 1985. The roof has caved in and the entire room is sinking into the deck below (above). Amazingly, some of the paneling — seen in the inset photograph opposite — is still visible on the aft wall (opposite, bottom). (Left) A visitor enjoys one of the gymnasium's mechanical horses prior to the ship's departure from Southampton. (Right) Author Jacques Futrelle poses on the Boat Deck in front of the gymnasium's arched windows.

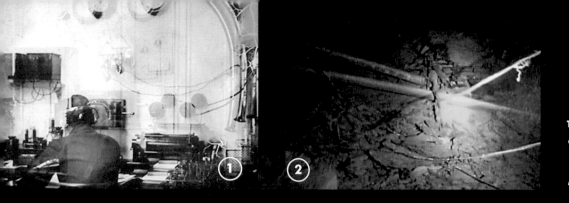

The Marconi and Silent Rooms

The *Titanic* carried one of the most powerful wireless telegraph stations afloat. In the Marconi Room, located amidships on the Boat Deck, Senior Operator Jack Phillips and his assistant Harold Bride transmitted and received signals. An adjacent soundproof room, appropriately named the Silent Room, contained the noisy spark-generating transmitting apparatus. The *Titanic*'s high-wattage transmitter, coupled with a large antenna elevated high above her stacks, enabled the spark to be carried hundreds, sometimes thousands, of miles. On the night of the disaster, all hopes for rescue hung on the distress calls frantically tapped out by Phillips and Bride.

(5) A composite of several images shows the remains of the Marconi Room, looking from starboard to port. In the distance stands a remnant of the wall that separated the two rooms. The white cables threading through the wall carried ship's electrical power to the transmitter motor. Just beyond the section of wall, part of the alternator (6) in the Silent Room is visible.

(7) This electrical distribution panel, once embedded in the forward wall of the Marconi Room, was connected to the ship's lighting circuit and supplied 100-volt direct current to run the Marconi transmitter motor. Close examination revealed that each fuse blew violently, distorting fuse clamps and scorching the wood underneath.

(2) Brass pneumatic tubing that once carried telegraph message forms between the Marconi Room and the Enquiry Office three decks below.

(3) A relay box for the Magneta automatic time system that actuated one of the clocks in the Marconi Room so that it always displayed local ship's time.

(4) A close-up of the High Frequency Spiral Inductance, which fell from the aft wall of the Silent Room after the pine paneling decayed.

(Above) In a computer-rendered cutaway, Jack Phillips sits working the key as he sends out calls for help while Harold Bride enters the Silent Room to adjust the spark.

(1) The only known photograph of the Marconi Room shows Harold Bride at the key.

The Silent Room

The Silent Room is the more intact of the two wireless rooms, evidently protected during the sinking by the thick walls designed to muffle the sound of the spark-generating machinery. Inside it stands the relatively intact transmitting apparatus, the device that gave the *Titanic* her voice — perhaps the most significant find of the expedition.

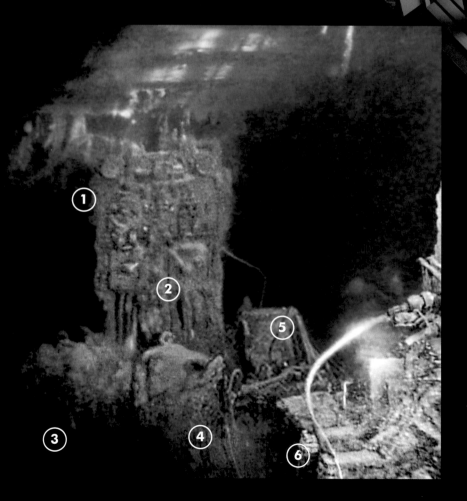

(Left) The presence of the switchboards (1) and regulators (2), with their heavy cast-iron foundations, has likely helped preserve this remnant of wall. The positions of the field regulator handles can be seen the way Bride left them as he tried to wring more power from the motor as the ship's power failed. The main switch on the D.C. panel (just to the left of the 2 in the cutaway above) is open, indicating that Phillips deliberately shut down the apparatus before abandoning the station.

(Above) The motor-generator set, comprising the alternator (3) and motor (4) mounted on a green bedplate, was rated for 5 kilowatts, one of the most powerful aboard ships in 1912. The disc discharger (5) produced a 60-Hz musical tone that raised *Titanic*'s call above the whispers of every other ship, including the *Olympic*, which carried a plain-spark discharger. The lead-lined teak cover to the discharger box was normally closed to help muffle the spark. The discovery of the open box in the wreck indicates that Harold Bride was adjusting the spark as the ship's power faded just before the end.

(Left) The remains of the transmitting jigger (7) lie virtually upright atop the condensers and commutator (6). The earth arrestor (8) and tuning lamp (9) are still connected into the circuit nearby. (Below) A view over the top of the motor-generator set toward the aft port corner of the Silent Room. On the night before the disaster, the two operators spent five hours in this corner disassembling the four condenser tanks (10) before Phillips eventually discovered and repaired a short inside the transformer (11). (Inset) This careful re-creation of the *Titanic*'s transmitting apparatus, based on data gathered during and after the expedition, matches the view below exactly.

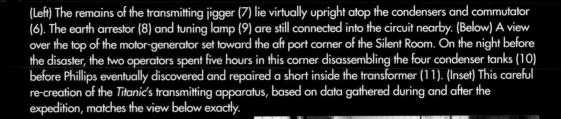

The Promenade Deck

(Below) Like eerie sunlight, shafts of light from MIR-2 pour through the windows of the starboard Promenade Deck. Although the deck is littered with fallen pipes and a thick carpeting of rusticles and other debris, the first-class stateroom windows and railings at right are still intact. (Inset) Looking aft on the promenade in 1912.

THIS DOOR FOR U
OF CREW ONLY

(Top) This well-preserved sign, found at the starboard forward end of
A Deck, is a ghostly reminder of the many crewmen who perished
while doing their duty the night of the disaster. (Inset) Inside the door
near which the sign hung were stairs that led up to the Boat Deck and
down to B Deck. Although the stairs are now missing, the handrail
remains nearby, still wrapped in the rope that afforded a better grip
in wet weather.

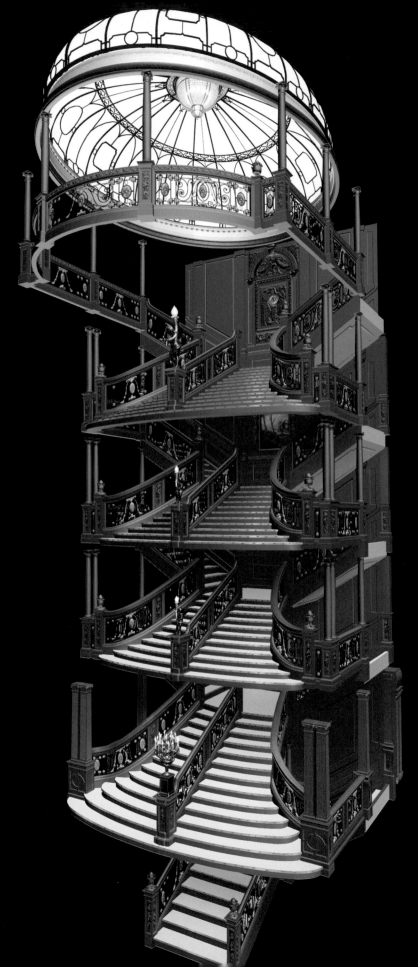

Titanic Revisited
The Grand Staircase

The forward first-class staircase (left) was one of the *Titanic*'s most opulent features. Crowned by a magnificent dome of wrought iron and glass and topped by an elaborately carved clock, the staircase extended from the Boat Deck (below), past the landing on A Deck (bottom) to E Deck. Today, all that remains in the wreckage is a gaping hole (right) and the steel foundation girders that supported the D-deck landing. The staircase itself, made entirely of oak, probably broke up and floated out of the ship during the sinking.

66

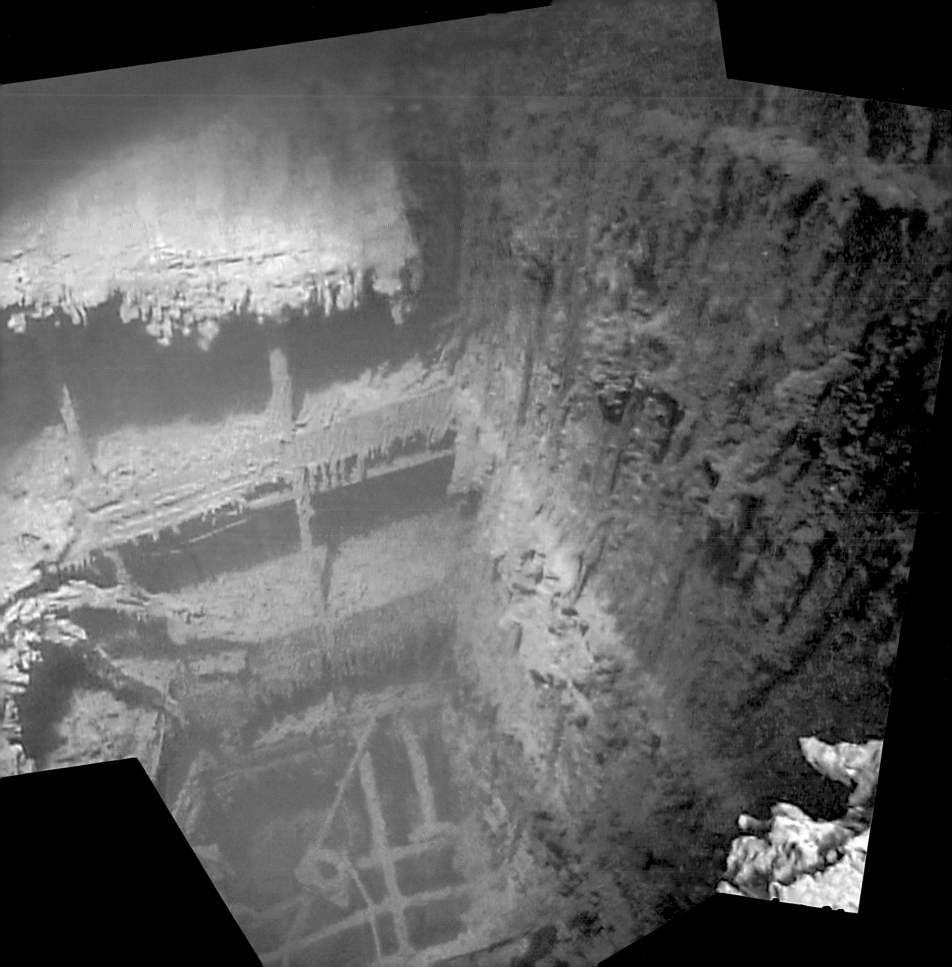

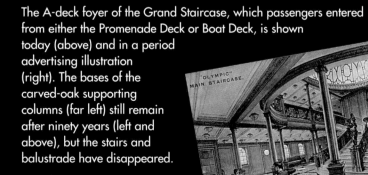

The A-deck foyer of the Grand Staircase, which passengers entered from either the Promenade Deck or Boat Deck, is shown today (above) and in a period advertising illustration (right). The bases of the carved-oak supporting columns (far left) still remain after ninety years (left and above), but the stairs and balustrade have disappeared.

Elegant crystal-beaded light fixtures that once hung from the foyer ceiling in gilded bases (far right) still remain in place (right), although many now dangle from electrical wires (below). Much of the woodwork surrounding the lights — and even some of the original white paint — has survived.

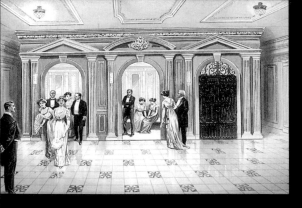

The Elevators

The *Titanic* and *Olympic* each had more elevators than any ocean liner afloat, including a bank of three for the exclusive use of first-class passengers (left). Under the rust-stained glass of the enunciator panel (below), the various deck levels that would be illuminated as the elevator traveled up and down are faintly visible. The wrought-iron grillwork of the doors (opposite, bottom) still

guards against entry to the elevator, just as it did in this 1912 photograph aboard the *Olympic* (inset). On each deck in first class hung two electrically lit sign boxes (far right) that guided passengers to the elevator behind the Grand Staircase. (Right) One of the brass boxes hangs from a ceiling, its opal glass probably knocked out or shattered during the sinking.

The Reception Room

With its exotic palms, plush carpeting, white-painted mahogany woodwork and cushioned wicker furniture, the beautiful Reception Room (inset, top) outside the Dining Saloon was so comfortable and inviting that passengers would sit for hours sipping coffee, socializing and listening to the ship's orchestra. (Inset, bottom) One of the planter boxes, seen in the right corner of the period photograph, still shows its ornate carving. (Opposite) Inside the Reception Room, Jake glides past the still-intact leaded-glass windows. The illustration (above) re-creates the elaborate detailing of this same section of the room.

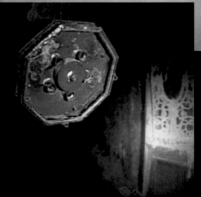

Elsewhere in the Reception Room, the decorative carved wood surrounding the steel columns (above) shows remarkably little deterioration, with paint still evident in the scalloped carving. The base of a gilt-brass light fixture that once held a delicate cut-glass bowl (right) now dangles empty from the ceiling (far right).

MIR-2's lights illuminate the intricate pattern (right) of one of the remarkably intact leaded-glass windows. In 1912, portholes — like the two just visible behind one of the Reception Room windows (below) — allowed natural light to enter the room.

The D-Deck
Entrance Vestibule

First-class passengers boarding the ship
passed through elaborate wrought-iron gates
and into the tiled entrance vestibule. A set of
doors, graced with panels of bronze grillwork
and glass, led into the Reception Room.
(Inset) A similar set of doors led from the
Reception Room to the Dining Saloon.
(Opposite) Although this door's glass has long
shattered, the bronze grillwork remains.
(Below) An illustration depicts the layout of
this area of the ship — including the entrance
vestibule, the D-deck foyer of the Grand
Staircase and the Reception Room. (Top, right)
One of the entrance vestibule doors, its grillwork
swung open and hanging from its hinges.
The bronze handle is still intact.

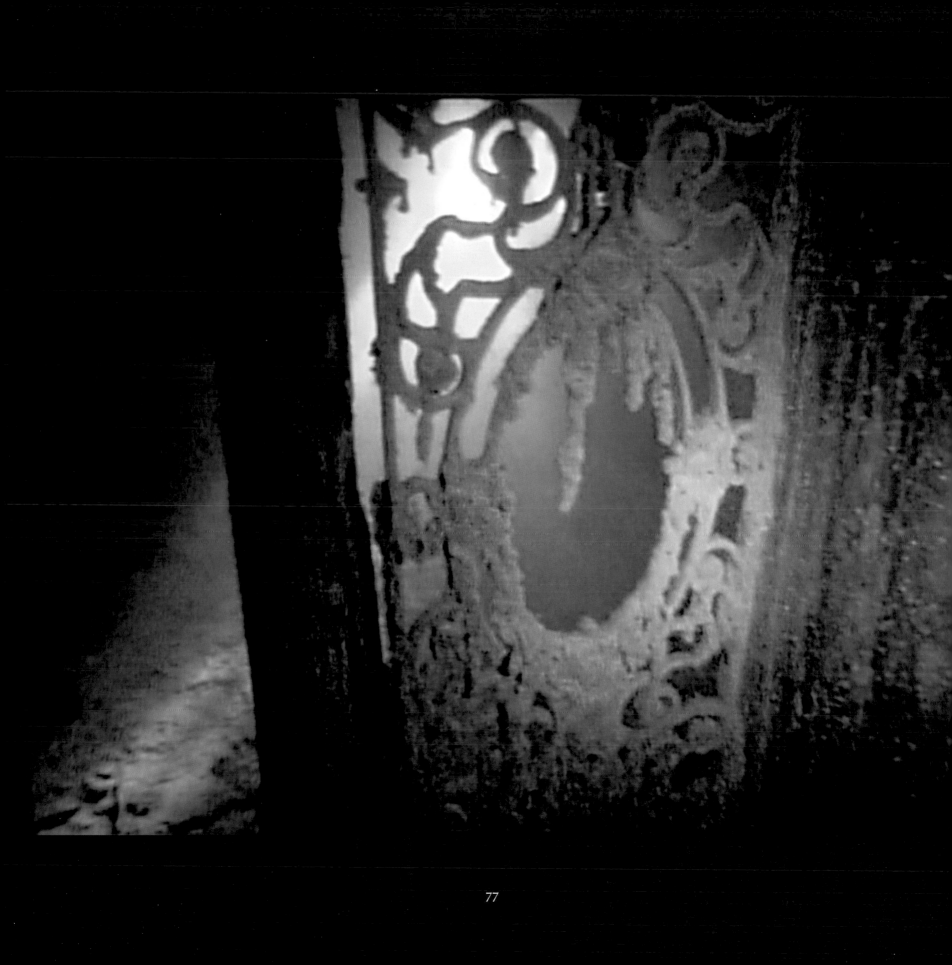

Because there is no known photograph of the two D-deck entrance vestibules, no one knew what the interior gates (left) looked like until Jim Cameron explored the area. The above illustration is based on expedition notes and on footage obtained during dives. (Below) Passengers board the *Olympic* through an exterior doorway. (Opposite) A wooden sideboard in the starboard entrance vestibule, now heaved away from the wall and fallen over, still contains china in the traditional White Star pattern. The service was likely used for serving tea and refreshments in the Reception Room.

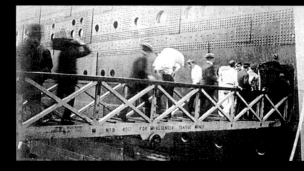

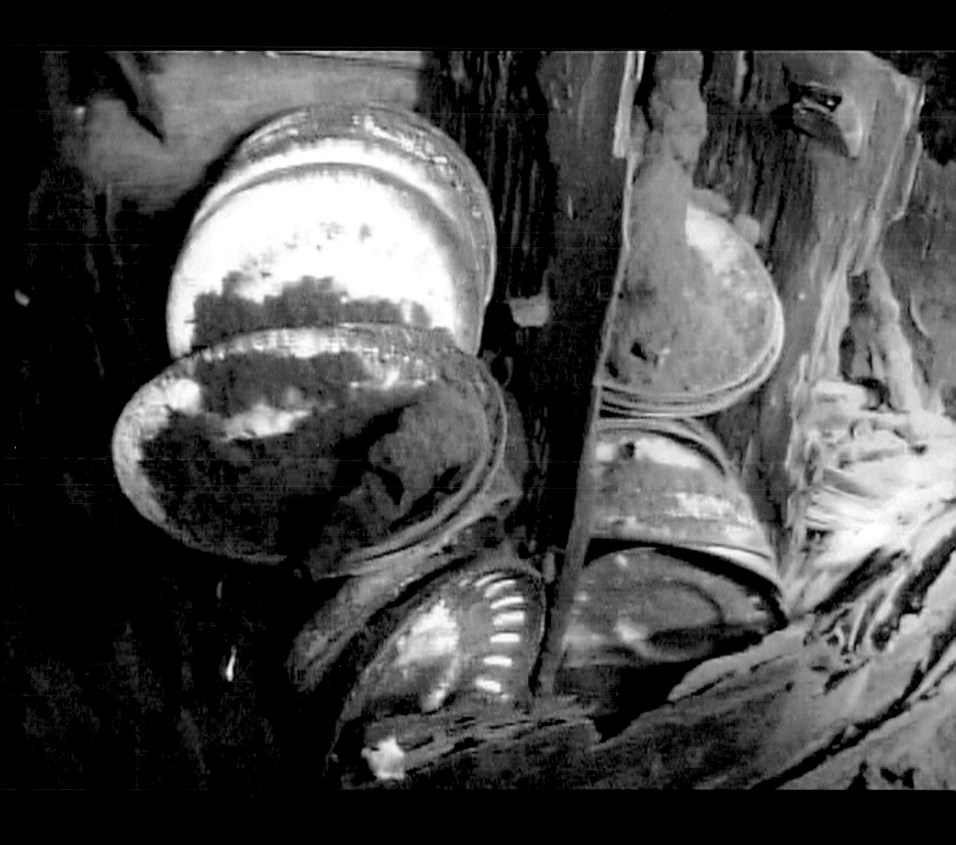

The Dining Saloon

Only the forward portion of the first-class Dining Saloon remains. The rest collapsed when the ship broke in two. (Below) Despite the nearby destruction, undamaged ornate leaded-glass windows still cover the portholes, and the cast-iron bases of tables rise from the debris and muck that litter the floor. (Inset) The handle of this fork from the era bears little stars, reminding diners that they were on a White Star liner.

(Inset) An alcove area in the Dining Saloon. (Top) The remains of one of the gilded brass light fixtures, which had been designed exclusively for use in the Dining Saloon. (Bottom) A rattail fish inspects the leaded-glass window and surrounding paneling.

Chapter Four *Exploring the* Titanic

When I made my first dive to the *Titanic,* it was early on in the expedition and Elwood and Jake weren't on board yet. At lunch on August 25, just a few days after we'd sent the MIRs down to the wreck for the first time, Jim unexpectedly announced that I would be diving the next day. I hadn't thought I would be going down so soon, since only two dives had been made so far. With some trepidation, I looked across the table at Ken. He had a "Gotcha!" look on his face — until Jim added, "And Ken, I want you in *MIR-2* with Lew."

My heart pounded for about two minutes. This was it. I was going down to the *Titanic.* When Jim had offered me the rare opportunity of accompanying him on his undersea explorations, I knew I couldn't pass it up, in spite of the risks. Nevertheless, I couldn't help asking myself whether I really wanted to be incarcerated in a cramped submersible as I descended two and a half miles to the bottom of the ocean. And did I really want to stay there for hours at a time, with only the sub's casing between me and 6,000 pounds per square inch of bone-crushing oceanic water pressure? As I steeled myself for the adventure, it was reassuring to know that at least I would be in *MIR-1* with Jim.

A storm front prevented us from diving the following day, leaving Lew Abernathy complaining that he'd brushed his teeth and had his hair French-braided for nothing. But after breakfast on Monday, August 27, we crowded into the MIR lab, where we learned that the weather was fine and the day's dive would go ahead. We also discovered that *Medusa* had blown a transformer and would have to stay behind on the *Eas* for repairs. Without the underwater chandelier system, Jim would have fewer lighting options than he had anticipated.

Out on the sunny deck, Bill Paxton interviewed me in front of *MIR-1* for a few moments, and I assured him that I now felt quite calm about the upcoming journey. Then I followed Jim as he climbed up to the hatch and stepped down to the seat below.

Before I had a chance to get comfortable, Jim was on the alert, cautioning me not to put my feet too far aft, where they would touch and possibly dislodge the cables connecting the cameras to the tape decks. There was floor space for only three legs — two of Anatoly's and one of Jim's. Jim tucked his other leg underneath him, while I lay on my side with my knees bent and my feet propped up on my part of the bench. Then Anatoly climbed in, closed the hatch and folded the ladder up against our only exit.

We were still getting settled when Jim pointed out calmly that we were being hoisted over the side. I hadn't felt the MIR move at all, but as I looked through my small porthole, I could see that we were swaying above the ocean. It was just after ten o'clock.

As we slowly descended to the bottom, Anatoly began doing equipment checks and discovered that the lighting boom

(Right) Before making a descent, each MIR was towed away from the side of the *Keldysh*. (Below) One of the submersibles begins the two-and-a-half-hour journey down to the wreck site, its manipulator arms and a viewport illuminated by the external lights. These will soon be turned off to save battery power.

just outside the portholes would go up and down but not left or right. This limited maneuverability would likely make filming a waste of time, so Jim, with his characteristic decisiveness, said the dive would have to be aborted. But Anatoly persevered and the equipment eventually responded to all commands. With that, we relaxed and settled down for the slow and dark journey to the bottom. Every hour, I was to call out the time and check to make sure the videotapes were still rolling as the interior cameras recorded our every move.

We were coming close to the ocean floor when Jim turned on the exterior lights and discovered that the matte box surrounding the camera lens was showing up in the camera image. The box, installed to stop light from hitting the lens from the side, was not meant to show up on camera, but once we were in the water, the refraction made it visible. So now, as we were approaching our destination, Jim had to decide once more whether or not to abort the dive. In the end, nothing more was said about terminating the operation. Jim later explained that he'd decided to keep pressing on, since the good lens would still produce useable footage. The shots just wouldn't be three-dimensional.

Suddenly, the blackness was broken as an image began to appear on the camera monitor. It was the bottom of the sea, looking smooth and gray. Millions of years of silting had created this soft-looking, uniform surface, broken only by an occasional bump or by a ghostly white rattail fish swimming by.

As we moved forward to find the ship, Anatoly jumped into action, switching constantly between the center, left, and right portholes. I propped myself up on my left elbow so I could see more clearly. Before long, the sonar revealed something large straight ahead, which in moments proved to be a huge piece of the ship's hull. It was red, evidence that it had been below the waterline, where red anti-fouling paint had been applied to prevent marine growth from attaching itself to the ship. As I noticed the long shadow cast by one edge of the hull, I realized that seeing the *Titanic* in photographs could never compare to viewing it in person. Only a face-to-face encounter could reveal its true dimensions.

Beyond the red hull fragment, the ocean was still a dark chasm, lit only by the MIR's beams. The overwhelming solitude was punctuated by a few more rattails and an occasional starfish splayed out like a lonely sculpture on the silty floor.

Then, just ahead of us rose a wall of steel — the starboard side of the *Titanic* — entrenched in the deep trough that still remained from the wreck's impact on the bottom ninety years before. Anatoly guided the MIR upward, and as we ascended through the murky waters, Jim began calling out the first few levels: F Deck, E Deck, D Deck. We were inches away from the hull, as close as the people in the

lifeboats had been when they were being lowered. I didn't realize it until later, but we were moving up the side of the ship in just about the same position as lifeboat No. 7 had descended. No. 7 had been the first to leave the ship, with only twenty-eight occupants on board. When we reached the first-class A-deck promenade, we began moving forward as we ascended up and over the Boat Deck. The deck struck me as being extremely wide — but I soon realized that it looked that way because the lifeboats were no longer encroaching on it.

There seemed to be a strong current, and Anatoly was working hard to maneuver against it. We drifted away from the ship for a few minutes as we moved slowly toward the bow,

but Anatoly found his way back. We settled down near the breakwater — designed to protect the deck from waves crashing over the bow — and waited there for the arrival of *MIR-2*.

As the minutes rolled by, we realized that the other sub was no longer responding to our calls. They'd radioed when they were twenty meters aft of the *Titanic*'s bow section, but now they'd fallen silent. We assumed that the ship itself, now lying between us, was interfering with the underwater acoustic communication system, known as UQC, that both submersibles used.

Finally, *MIR-2* radioed to say that they were on the starboard Boat Deck beside the davit for lifeboat No. 1, so Jim instructed Anatoly to head that way. In spite of our pilot's

The forward davit, where lifeboat No.1 and collapsible C were launched, is the only one still standing on the starboard side.

best efforts, however, the positioning did not go smoothly. Jim wanted *MIR-2* to light the Boat Deck from off to one side as we drifted aft along it, but sometimes we were too high or too low. Then *MIR-2* would drift away from its correct position when we were ready to start filming. Sometimes the lights from *MIR-2* shone directly into *MIR-1*'s camera lens. Jim reacted patiently to all this, but once, when I looked over at him, he rolled his eyes and said that getting a good shot was "like working with a pick and shovel."

At one point during our filming, Jim discovered that the tapes for the 3-D cameras had run out. I'd become so absorbed in looking at the *Titanic* that I'd completely forgotten my job of calling out each hour to make sure we

stopped and checked them. "Don, you're supposed to be watching this!" Jim snapped. I was using a timer I'd been given, setting it for three-hour increments, but I didn't realize that the 3-D cameras had been started at a different time than the interior miniature "lipstick" cameras. Had I known that, I would have used the timer on my watch to track the second set of tapes. Although Jim's frustration at not getting every pass captured on tape was obvious, he soon spoke in more moderate tones and laid blame on the person he'd tasked with obtaining a second timer.

Our next goal was to film on the port side of the Boat Deck We crossed over the top of the ship, above a gaping hole

The lights from *MIR-2* cast a ghostly glow on the portside Boat Deck near the officers' quarters and the Marconi Room.

where a funnel had once risen, and hovered around the Marconi Room, near where the Grand Staircase had been. The forwardmost davit on this part of the deck was intact, and we asked *MIR-2* to light it up, along with the deck space around it.

As we were filming, a light on the control panel came on and an alarm sounded, but Anatoly just turned it off and we continued. Jim, who seemed to know every instrument in the submersible by heart, explained that the warning indicated water in our hydraulics system, but the problem was not life threatening. I told him I assumed it wasn't dangerous or he wouldn't be setting up the next shot. Jim smiled and said not to be so sure about that.

We proceeded to an open area on the Boat Deck near the entrance to the Grand Staircase, where the *Titanic*'s musicians had played on the night of the sinking. Jim now tried something different. We rested above the Boat Deck while *MIR-2*, out of frame, shone its lights along the deck and drifted toward us. As *MIR-2* came nearer, its lights revealed more and more of the deck and its adjacent bulkhead while, in the background, the areas that had been illuminated moments before fell back into darkness.

With the hydraulics alarm repeatedly going off, we ended the dive. As we floated back up toward the surface, Jim wrapped a towel around his neck, placed a blanket between his head and the wall, and fell asleep. Very seldom on the

expedition did he have down time to stop and rest, and this was one of his few chances to do so. I lay on my back with my left foot on Anatoly's seatback and my right leg resting against the cold hull of the submersible. Condensation trickled down the inside of the MIR, and though I knew it was harmless, I couldn't help thinking about leaks. I also tried not to look at the hatch. For some reason, it reminded me of how much water pressure was on the other side.

The ascent seemed to go much more slowly than the trip down, although they both take exactly the same amount of time. But shortly after 5:30 P.M., the water began to grow brighter, and before we knew it, we were bouncing around on the surface.

When I emerged from the MIR, it was still daylight, though the shadows were lengthening. The skies were clear, with only a few wispy clouds in the distance. After sitting more or less immobile in the sub for so many hours, my legs were shaky, so I climbed down the ladder carefully and landed on deck, ecstatic that the trip had gone so well.

Jim, of course, wasted no time in taking charge of the filming as soon as he stepped out of the submersible. He'd been restrained in the MIR, but now he made it clear that he was furious about the matte box showing up on camera. Then he started barking at the guys who were operating the crane holding a 3-D camera out over the side of the *Keldysh*. Before long, they were using it to film *MIR-2* being hoisted

aboard, its weight making the ship list to starboard. No matter where you were on the *Keldysh,* you always knew when a MIR was being brought aboard or lowered over the side — rooms would start slanting in that direction and unsecured objects would sometimes slide off tables.

On September 9, two days after Elwood's breakdown, Jim called me to his room to tell me I'd be diving again the next day. It would be my second dive to the wreck. I'd be in *MIR-1* again, and *MIR-2* would carry Charlie Pellegrino, a paleontologist interested in rusticles who had written two books about the *Titanic,* and John Broadwater, a marine archaeologist with the National Oceanographic and Atmospheric Administration. This time, we'd cover the stern and the debris field. This scenario sounded excellent, since it would allow me to see areas I'd not encountered the first time. I had just returned to the cabin Ken and I shared when Jim rushed in and asked Ken which D-deck entry door was open on the port side of the *Titanic.* He was hatching a plot to rescue Elwood by somehow taking the ROV out the side of the ship.

After the model meeting, Jim arrived at our door again to break the news that he'd changed his plans and I would not be diving. Instead, he'd take ROV pilot Jeff Ledda on this dive and I would go down to the wreck with Ken the next day, the 11th. This was the last dive before our return to St. John's, so Jim wanted to go for broke and try to film everything he could. He sat on Ken's bed, talking with us about the development of the ROVs and his plans to clean up as much fiber-optic cable from the ship as he could, rather than waiting for it to dissolve on its own during the next five years, as it was designed to do. Over the course of the last three dives, hundreds of feet of tether had spooled out of the two ROVs, and it was now strung about the ship. Jim also spoke of his own work habits, admitting that he performs best in "crisis mode" and that, for him, everything else is "sleep walking." He always sets his goals above what can be achieved. Anything less, he said, might make him stop once his goal was reached. By setting his sights too high, he has a better chance of reaching the limits of his abilities.

At the production meeting on the 11th, Jim went over the day's shots and his idea for rescuing Elwood. He admitted he was planning some of it right then and there because he hadn't had time to do so after his return to the surface the day before. And he expected to do still more planning on the way to the bottom. Jim had gone on all seven dives, but this one was happening much faster than the others had.

That morning, the sea was the calmest it had been in days, and the weather was warm. As always, *MIR-1*, with Jim, Jeff, and Anatoly on board, was launched first. Just after 11:30 A.M., Ken, Genya, and I in *MIR-2* were hoisted over the side and lowered into the water.

We'd been descending for just over an hour when John David Cameron suddenly called his brother over the UQC radio. Since the communication system was acoustic-based, we could hear it as well. The message came across as a series of nouns, and it struck me that it was some kind of code.

"*Keldysh, MIR-1*," Jim called back. "Do not understand. Over."

John David repeated the message, and Jim repeated it back to him. John David then told us that all air traffic had been stopped.

"Copy you, *Keldysh, Keldysh, MIR-1*," Jim responded. "Copy you. Understand. Terrorist activity, World Trade Center. Air travel stopped. Over."

I could only think of the 1993 bombing of the New York World Trade Center but wondered why air travel would be stopped. What was the connection?

Ken looked at Genya and me and asked, "Why are they telling us that now?"

"What?" Genya asked, not understanding what we were hearing.

"What is it?"

"I don't know," Ken replied. "Is it a joke?"

Jim also had questions. "*Keldysh, MIR-1*," he called. "Do not understand. Are you recommending we abort dive? Over."

"*MIR-1, Keldysh*. Do not, I say again, do not abort dive.

Over," John David answered.

Again, no one gave any indication as to why this information was being passed along.

"He said there was terrorist activity at the World Trade Center and all flights have been stopped," I repeated to Ken and Genya. I acknowledged that it was certainly serious and thought to myself, with disappointment, that this news would surely put a damper on the entire dive.

"*Keldysh, MIR-1*, affirmative," Jim answered. "You will keep us posted. We will continue dive. Over and out."

Now, in the time remaining in our descent, we could only wonder what was going on.

Over in *MIR-1*, Anatoly, like Genya, had not really paid attention, assuming that if it involved him, a message would have been communicated in Russian as well.

"Tolya," Jim said, addressing Anatoly by his nickname, "terrorists attacked the World Trade Center."

"What?" Anatoly asked, perplexed.

"Terrorists attacked the World Trade Center. All of the U.S. is on alert. All air traffic has been stopped."

"Oh, I see," he replied. Like the rest of us, he knew there was nothing he could do.

Jim then turned to Jeff, the ROV pilot, and said, "Kind of puts things in perspective. We're poking through this ninety-year-old wreckage and the real world carries on."

We grew quiet, Genya assuming what I called his "headache position," placing his head in one hand as he rested. He'd been up late the night before doing maintenance on the MIR after the previous day's dive.

Suddenly, Anatoly radioed over the UQC in Russian, and Genya took a quick look at the sonar. "See that?" he said, tapping the screen.

"Yes," I replied.

"It's *MIR-1*."

He leaned forward toward the controls, and I looked out my porthole. Just outside, we could see three lights no more than forty feet away. We were apparently spiraling in our descent, for *MIR-1* soon spun away to port and out of our view. Genya worked frantically to power up the thrusters of *MIR-2* while talking back and forth with Anatoly to make sure the two submersibles didn't collide. Finally, they agreed on who would head in which direction, and the two MIRs moved away from each other. When the crisis was over, I joked to my submates that in an ocean the size of the Atlantic, one wouldn't expect to run into someone one knew. Though I was trying to make light of the situation, everyone was aware that we'd had a close call.

As always, the two MIRs had been launched half an hour apart to prevent a collision, but Genya explained that *MIR-1* had probably turned on its thrusters occasionally to recover from drifting too far away. By doing so, it had likely slowed its descent and moved laterally instead. No pilot would have been prepared for this, since the likelihood of such a close encounter was extremely remote. In the fourteen years the two sub-mersibles had been in existence, no one remembered such a thing happening.

With the excitement of our near-collision, the distressing news from the *Keldysh* was shelved and we nearly forgot about it altogether as we reached the bottom and focused on our mission. Looking out at the ocean floor, I found that I had a much better view than on my first dive. One enormously thick starfish lay on the silt, surrounded by a number of smaller relatives.

When *MIR-1* reported that they had reached the site, we powered up and proceeded forward. Ken looked out his porthole at one point and told me to do the same. I could see nothing, but when I looked again a moment later, there, suddenly looming before us, was the bow of the *Titanic*. Instead of coming up on the side of the hull, as we had on my first dive, we were now approaching the very forepeak itself, rising out of the silt. We lifted off the bottom and rose up over it.

As we moved slowly over the bow and toward the superstructure, the ship's copper- and amber-colored rusticles glowed

(Below) Rusticles now shroud the fallen foremast that once held the crow's nest where lookout Frederick Fleet first spotted the deadly iceberg. (Opposite, left) Genya carefully maneuvers *MIR-2* over the gaping well that once held the splendid Grand Staircase. (Opposite, right) Jake carefully makes his way down to the Reception Room, where Elwood awaits rescue nearby.

even more beautifully than they had on my first dive. The 3-D camera's lights on *MIR-1* had caused more backscatter, but now the details of the wreck seemed much sharper. As we approached the fallen mast, the cracks between its plates were clearly visible. Nearby, the arms of the cargo cranes stood high above the deck, their dark shadows falling starkly below them. What was under there? We rose up over the bridge and, following Jim's instructions, headed aft on the port side. Jim wanted us to face forward and rest at the edge of the Boat Deck with our boom light hanging over the side. This, he said, is where we would return once Elwood had been retrieved.

But first, we had to get into position for the rescue. Jim had us move over the Grand Staircase and aim our lights down it. It was difficult finding a place to hover where we didn't risk teetering into the stairwell or falling through a decaying roof — but Genya is extremely accomplished and knows the wreck intimately, so we finally found a suitable spot. Then, under our illumination, Jake descended down the staircase opening to D Deck, headed for the entrance vestibule.

Once Jake had left the stairwell area, still tethered to *MIR-1* by his long fiber-optic cable, we moved out over the side of the ship and down to the open D-deck entry door on the port side. Our mission was to illuminate it. Genya positioned us up-current a short distance from the door and did so. As we drifted past the door, he would keep the light aimed inside. Once we began to get too far past, he would motor back to his original spot, all the while keeping the light aimed in. I was amazed at his ability to manage both these tasks simultaneously. With our light pouring in the doorway, Jake's pilot would always have a point of reference.

This high-tech twenty-first-century rescue effort, played out against the ruins of the highest technology of a century before, relied on one astonishingly low-tech device for its eventual success. When Jim first decided to attempt the operation, the ROV team had begun looking for a way to hook Elwood to Jake and drag the injured 'bot out of the wreck. But it was Lewis Abernathy who came up with the solution: a coat hanger attached to the "healthy" 'bot, which would spear the wire mesh covering Elwood's propellers. Jake could then tow Elwood toward the light in the distance, which marked the escape route.

The plan seemed relatively simple, but many things could go wrong. Jake did not have the maneuverability he needed to connect easily to Elwood. He would have to head-butt the other ROV to secure the coat-hanger "spear" in the mesh around Elwood's propellers. If Jake missed and the spear hit a more solid part of Elwood, the tip might bend and become unusable for a second try. To make matters worse, Elwood's tether spool might have been damaged by the battery explosion. If that was the case and Jake became irreversibly connected to Elwood, Elwood's tether wouldn't spool out and both ROVs would be lost. As a precaution, a cutting

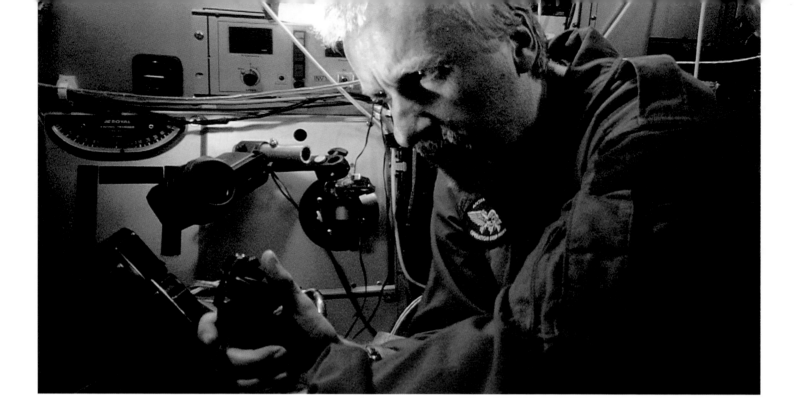

device was added to Jake so the lanyard holding the spear could be severed if necessary.

We'd prepared for the rescue as well as we could, but now that we were about to begin, we all knew we could end up with a more severe catastrophe than the one we were trying to repair. Unfortunately, it was our only hope, so we started the operation as planned. Slowly, Jake moved through the darkness of the entrance vestibule.

Not surprisingly, Elwood was still resting against the ceiling where he had died, his bright green surface easily reflecting Jake's lights among the silt, rusticles, and time-darkened paneling.

"Where, oh, where is my little 'bot now?" Jim murmured in *MIR-1* as he and Jeff concentrated on maneuvering Jake closer to the invalid.

"All right, time to go in for the kill," he said as they came closer.

"That looks good," he went on, "yaw right…go for a drive and see if he comes with us."

Jeff and Jim tried several times before they finally managed to hook Elwood. They knew they'd succeeded when the hook was no longer visible in the upper left corner of the monitor. There was also a different feel to the controls.

"I'm yawing," Jim said, still sounding cool, but he, like Jeff, knew the significance of the moment.

Jeff told Jim to fly Jake closer to the floor, since Elwood was so buoyant that he would otherwise drag along the ceiling at the end of the tether, bringing down rusticle clouds and hiding Elwood from his rescuers.

Jim then aimed Jake at the light coming through the distant doorway and began piloting in that direction. But his efforts were frustrated. "We're stuck — like hitting a wall — hung up. Solid. Absolutely solid." Jim covered his undoubted frustration with his measured commentary.

Elwood's tether wouldn't pay out because the battery had damaged the spool. No matter how much thrust Jim

(Opposite) The tension is evident on Jim Cameron's face as he deftly manipulates the joystick that controls Jake during the final moments of the rescue operation. (Right) Jake emerges triumphantly from the *Titanic*'s D-deck entry door with Elwood in tow.

gave, the 'bot would not go forward any more. So Jim backtracked and tried again, but with no success. Over and over he tried to move Jake, but Elwood was obviously stuck.

Finally, Jim concluded there was nothing more they could do, so he told Jeff to cut the connection between the two 'bots. For some reason, however, the cutting mechanism failed. The two men worked at trying to sever the lanyard, but this also ended in frustration.

Then Jim tried towing Elwood toward the door once again, this time giving Jake a running start and pushing him to full speed.

"Hey! We're going!" Jim exclaimed in *MIR-1*.

Amazingly, Elwood was moving at last and approaching the lights of *MIR-2*, which were now beaming brightly into Jim's field of vision. "*MIR-2*, *MIR-2*, tilt your lights down. Tilt your lights down."

"Copy that," I said from *MIR-2*. "Tilting it down."

At first, we saw only Jake heading toward the doorway, but then we spied Elwood coming right behind. It was a robot parade. "Oh, my God," Ken exclaimed, "he got it!"

"Tell him to take a visual on us and see if we have Elwood," Jim instructed Jeff.

"Do you see Elwood?" Jeff radioed over to us in *MIR-2*.

"It looks great. It's beautiful!" I said, but they didn't understand.

"DO YOU SEE ELWOOD?" Jeff repeated.

"Yes, we do!" I replied.

"Got him!"

Incredibly, Elwood was on his way home — and Jake was undamaged.

Back on board the *Keldysh*, I climbed out of the submersible into a world of bustling activity. Elwood was finally home. He was covered with stinky black slime, but he was safe at last. Bill welcomed me back on deck, and I started telling our exciting tale to Michael Maltzman and Eric Schmitz of the ROV team. Eric had a very sober look on his face, which didn't match my enthusiasm, but I didn't think to wonder why until Ken climbed out of *MIR-2* and arrived on deck.

That's when Bill told us what had happened.

"Attack on the United States," he said grimly. "The World Trade Center towers — two separate hijacked commercial jets." Eric's wife had been only a few blocks from Ground Zero. Even though he'd learned hours earlier that she was safe, it had been a rough day for him. And now we were told that as many as twenty thousand others were believed dead. It was just too much to absorb. Passenger jets hijacked. The twin towers completely demolished. The Pentagon hit.

I had left one world behind and returned to another that was completely changed. I was in a state of disbelief.

As the ROVs explored the *Titanic*'s interior, their lights picked out brass beds, washstands, wall racks and other fittings that stood out among murky piles of debris. But where, we wondered, were the steamer trunks and leather bags? In the debris field, luggage and shoes have survived surprisingly well — perhaps because the tannic acid in the leather prevents destructive organisms from devouring it, or because the stronger current outside the ship sweeps the luggage clean of anything harmful.

We also noticed that the only remains of a door would be the portion with the metal knob and push plate. Metal items such as bedframes, door knobs, and hinges emit the tiniest of electrical discharges, which irritates the undersea creatures that eat the wood and material around them. As a result, some fabric draped over an electrical wire still moves gently with the current, and a piece of cloth lying across a footboard looks as if someone had hung a jacket there — and never returned to put it on.

(Above) Second-class passengers stroll on the Boat Deck while the *Titanic* lies at anchor off Queenstown, Ireland. (Left) First-class passenger Lily Odell stands between her two brothers, Richard and Stanley May, while her son Jack poses with his camera. (Opposite) Made of brass with gilded inlays, this elegant headboard in a first-class stateroom on A Deck gleams in the light cast by the ROV Jake.

Ghostly Staterooms

(Above) As this White Star advertisement shows, even second-class accommodation on the *Titanic* far surpassed 1912 standards.

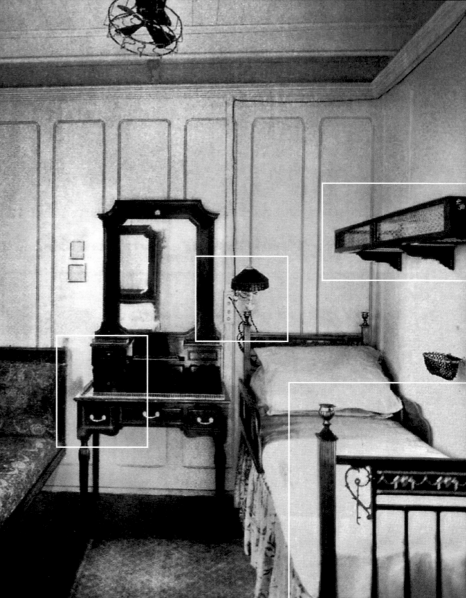

(Above) Furnishings in this comfortable A-deck first-class stateroom included a sofa, mahogany dressing table and brass bed with mounted gimbal lamp. (Left) Amid the remains of another stateroom, a lamp lies on the floor by the headboard at left, its cord still connected to an outlet. Although the dressing table has collapsed, the intact open lower drawer still sports its decorative brass pull.

(Right) Now covered with silt, this mahogany luggage rack with its wire-mesh sides — seen opposite — kept a passenger's belongings stowed securely away, particularly in rough weather. (Below) One A-deck stateroom contained an ornate footboard with tattered bedding still in place and the shreds of what might once have been clothing thrown over it. The fabric was likely protected from decay by direct contact with the metal of the bed.

(Above) One of the most exciting finds of the expedition was an upright wash cabinet, seen here from the back. The pine wall behind it has long since disintegrated, but — amazingly — an upright carafe and glass have survived in their specially constructed low wooden holders. The fact that the glass is right side up indicates that the stateroom's occupant likely took a drink of water the day of the sinking. A white-jacketed ship's steward routinely provided clean glasses and fresh water each morning. In the archival photograph at left, the glasses are turned upside down, ready for use. (Bottom right) A deck steward carries refreshments.

To maximize space in the cabins, many of the *Titanic*'s first-class staterooms had wash cabinets with "tip basins" that could be folded down for use (left). When the basin was folded back into the cabinet, the water would drain out the lip at the back. (Opposite, top) Two of these basins are visible still folded up into the cabinet. (Below) As much of the wood inside the ship has decayed over the years, the weight of the heavy porcelain basins has caused the cabinets to collapse onto the floor.

(Right) This photograph shows how Henry Harper's first-class stateroom on D Deck would have looked. (Below) The spacious portholes of the first-class staterooms on C and D Decks could be turned sideways on center pivots, directing a breeze into the room. This porthole, found in the Harper stateroom, may have opened on impact with the bottom — or been left ajar by the room's occupant. (Opposite, top) *Titanic* passengers, many in bowler hats, wait to board at Queenstown. (Inset) A 1912 bowler hat.

Henry Harper's Hat

Preserved amid the wreckage of Stateroom D-33 was a bowler hat (bottom right) that likely belonged to Henry Sleeper Harper, grandson of one of the founders of the New York publishing firm Harper and Brothers. The forty-seven-year-old Harper had boarded the *Titanic* with his wife, an Egyptian manservant and a Pekingese dog named Sun Yat Sen. In an account he wrote for his family's magazine, *Harper's Weekly*, Harper described seeing the iceberg pass by his porthole. When ship's doctor William O'Loughlin assured him nothing was wrong, Harper blurted out, "Damn it, man, this ship has struck an iceberg! How can you say there's nothing serious?" He was appalled at the lack of organization during the sinking. No officer directed them where to go, and it was only from other passengers that he heard that lifejackets were to be donned. Once on the water in boat No. 3, Harper had to show a crewman how to use the tiller properly. All four members of the Harper party were saved, including the Pekingese.

(Above) This wooden door, found in first-class stateroom D-27, still has its mahogany push plate and metal doorknob. A matching door and doorknob from the *Olympic* are shown in the insets at left. In the background looms a still-intact mirror that was once mounted on a wardrobe.

Above many headboards in first class were an electrical outlet, two light switches and a call button (seen in the two photographs top and bottom, and in the archival at bottom left). First-class passenger Hugh Rood of Denver may have been reading in bed in this stateroom, A-32, at the time of the collision. His lamp, once mounted on the wall above his bed, has now fallen and is teetering across his headboard (top left), its cord still plugged into the outlet.

The stateroom assigned to fashion journalist Edith Rosenbaum (below) included a marble wash cabinet of the period (right) — its frame, mirror and marble sink with plated fittings still remarkably intact (opposite). A drinking glass still sits in the rack on the right. To the far right of the cabinet, the etched privacy glass inside her window now leans into the room.

Edith Rosenbaum's Mirror

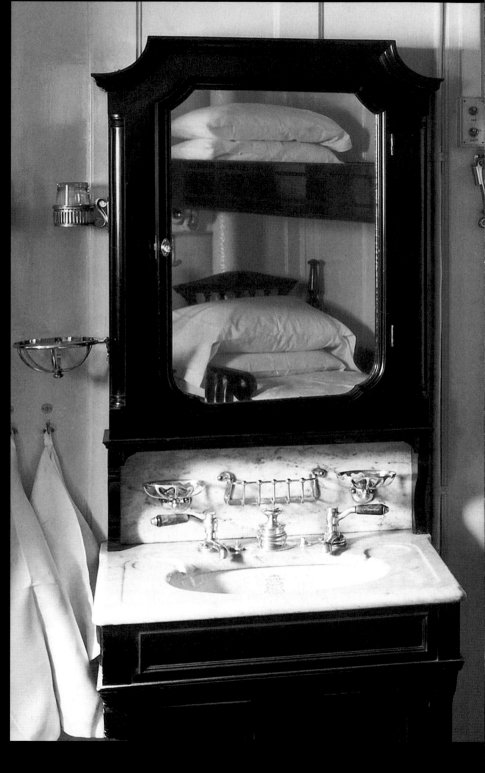

It seems appropriate that the best-preserved washstand mirror seen inside the *Titanic* was in stateroom A-11, occupied by one of the most style-conscious and colorful women aboard the *Titanic*. Thirty-three-year-old Edith

Rosenbaum, the daughter of a wealthy Cincinnati merchant, had been residing in Paris since 1907, where she wrote for the fashion magazine *Women's Wear Daily*. On the night of the disaster, Edith approached lifeboat No. 11 swathed in furs and complaining of all she had left behind. When told she could not take belongings with her, she refused to enter the lifeboat without the musical toy pig she clutched in her hands. A frustrated crewman took the pig from her and tossed it into the boat. Following it was not so easy, as Edith was wearing a hobble skirt and needed the help of several men to hoist her over the rail and into the boat. Edith Rosenbaum (later Russell) lived until 1975. Just days before the sixty-third anniversary of the *Titanic* disaster, she passed away in London at the age of ninety-six.

J. Bruce Ismay's Parlour Suite

Each of the four parlour suites aboard the *Titanic* and the *Olympic* boasted two bedrooms, private baths, wardrobe rooms and a large sitting room. The *Titanic*'s B-deck parlour suites also had private promenades. White Star managing director J. Bruce Ismay occupied the suite on the port side of the ship — although how much time he spent enjoying his lavish accommodations may never be known. During the first days at sea, Ismay circulated throughout the ship, socializing and seeking improvements that he could incorporate into the design of the next White Star liner, *Gigantic*.

Unfortunately, he did not always make a good impression on those who saw him. Mrs. Elizabeth Lines of Paris, who overheard him talking to Captain Smith about the ship's run, thought him emphatic and dictatorial. Colonel Archibald Gracie, who was very conscious of societal proprieties, noted during the sinking that Ismay "wore a day suit, and, as usual, was hatless." Kind or dictatorial, properly dressed or not, these impressions of Ismay were insignificant compared to how the world saw him after he had clambered aboard collapsible C and saved himself from the shipwreck — leaving over fifteen hundred of his passengers and crew to die.

The B-deck port parlour suite that J. Bruce Ismay occupied was decorated in the Louis Seize style — shown (opposite) in the counterpart suite on board the *Titanic*'s sister ship *Olympic*. Today, most of the elaborate furnishings and woodwork are gone, leaving only a huge layer of debris on the floor. Still recognizable, however, is the marble faux fireplace (below), with its bronze decorative detail (right).

The parlour suite's private promenade had a traditionally English, half-timbered, Elizabethan decor (inset, top). Looking down the length of the promenade (inset, bottom), little is left that is immediately recognizable. (Below) One of the surviving details is this section of preserved decorative woodwork, now fallen into the debris.

It is doubtful that Ismay took full advantage of the promenade deck, and it is unlikely that he entertained there at all, despite the tables and comfortable lounge chairs that were provided (opposite, top inset). In fact, on only one known occasion did Ismay invite guests back to his parlour suite — for an after-dinner game of bridge in the spacious sitting room. (Below) The glass is missing from the twin windows to Ismay's bedroom, seen from the promenade deck, but the frames themselves are plainly visible.

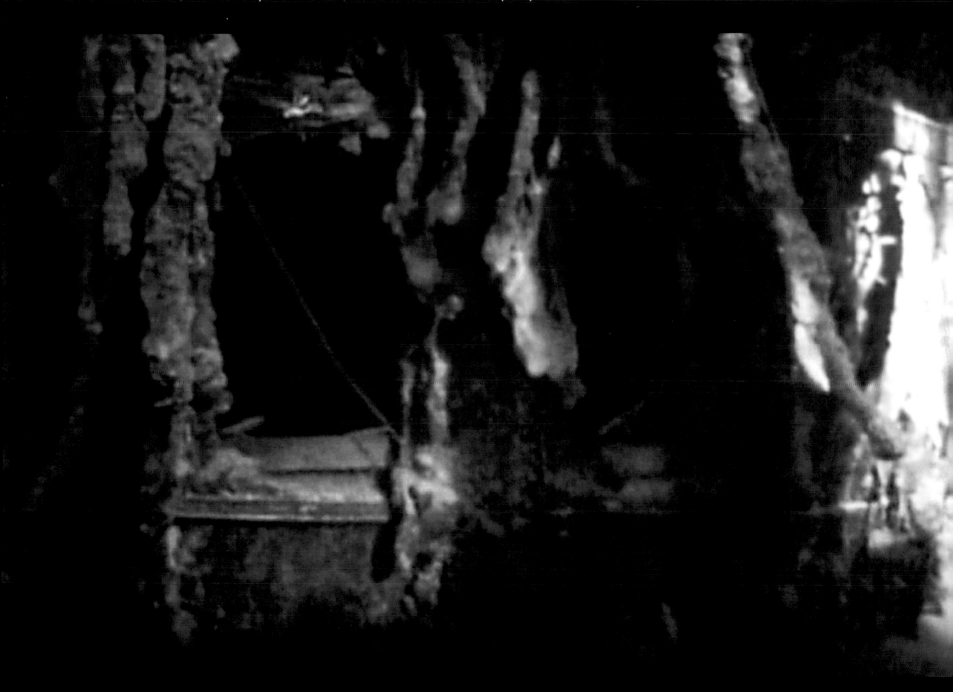

Chapter Six *From Disaster to Triumph*

As we headed back to St. John's under darkened skies on Wednesday, September 12, a cloud of gloom and uncertainty hung over the *Keldysh*. Our Russian hosts were extremely sympathetic as we tried to come to terms with the catastrophe in New York, Pennsylvania, and Washington — and although no dive was taking place that morning, a MIR meeting was called. As we clustered around the work table in the MIR lab, Anatoly read a message of condolence sent by Professor Sergey Lappo, the director of the institute that operated the ship: "…We condemn those who are responsible for those inhuman deeds," he read. "Your…[misfortune] is ours as well. We all must do everything…to stop the terrorism. There must be no room in the world for…creatures who have no care for…human lives. We share the sorrow and indignation of the American people."

To our surprise, the Russians had found a recording somewhere on board of Ray Charles singing "God Bless America," and they warmed our hearts by playing it over the loudspeaker in the dining room.

Overwhelmed by the tragedy at home, I kept thinking how trivial our mission to the *Titanic* had now become. All along, we'd felt that what we were doing was of great historical importance. Then this horrible event happened and our mission seemed frivolous, a distraction. What was the point of studying an old wreck whose victims were no longer suffering when the lives of innocent people were being torn apart right now in a disastrous attack that had struck America to its very core?

That afternoon, a pod of dolphins kept pace with the *Keldysh*, perhaps descendants of the very dolphins that had followed the *Carpathia* the day after the *Titanic* tragedy. In the coming days, as I struggled to adjust to what had happened, parallels between the two disasters began to emerge in my mind. The *Titanic* and the World Trade Center towers were both engineering marvels of their time. The two towers had been designed to withstand the impact of a 707 aircraft — but still they fell. The *Titanic* had been designed to stay afloat with its first four compartments flooded, but not with five. The people killed in both disasters included many from the upper echelons of society, but with them died hundreds who lived less public lives. The *Titanic*, of course, was not deliberately destroyed, and its victims were not intentionally murdered, but both events were met with outrage and disbelief — and the tragedies would remain indelibly etched on the collective memory of the world.

With air travel banned all over the United States, innumerable international flights had been rerouted to Canada, and about seventeen thousand travelers had been stranded in St. John's. A rumor went around the *Keldysh* that this applied to shipping as well, which meant we would not be able to enter the harbor if it was full of diverted vessels. But we sailed right into port the next morning and berthed at the

(Right) A view of the harbor at St. John's, Newfoundland, from the top of Signal Hill. It was on this hilltop in 1901 that Guglielmo Marconi received the first transatlantic wireless radio message. (Below) In a rare quiet moment, Ken Marschall, left, Bill Paxton, right, and Jim Cameron reflect on two tragedies — September 11 and the *Titanic* disaster.

northern end — exactly where we'd been when we'd first departed in August. From the decks of the *Keldysh*, St. John's looked unchanged, the skies above filled with wispy clouds. However, once we were ashore, the effect of the events in America was obvious. The sidewalks were crowded with people, and the few major hotels were overflowing with stranded travelers of all ages and nations. Mattresses had been thrown down on the floors of reception areas outside the banquet rooms, and the rooms themselves were wall-to-wall with mattresses and bedding. Signs announced that lunch would be served at the nearby convention center.

Jim had been expecting to meet up with another team in St. John's, which would accompany him to the wreck of the *Bismarck* to take footage that would become part of his documentary. But the *Bismarck* experts had also been grounded, so it seemed futile to go on and investigate that wreck. Jim knew that many on the *Titanic* team wanted to leave to be with their families, yet ending the expedition completely would not be helpful either, since most of us had no way of getting home. As only eight of the twelve planned dives had actually been made, the best option, Jim decided, was to return to the *Titanic* to complete the remaining four. He invited everyone to go back with him. My immediate choices were either to board the *Keldysh* again or, as far as I knew, sleep on the floor of the gymnasium at a local high school. I chose the *Keldysh*.

Once we were over the initial shock, our *Titanic* work became important to us again. I began to see the expedition from a new perspective now that I understood even more how the world had been affected by the news of the *Titanic*'s sinking. I also realized that the ship's victims should not be forgotten just because a greater, more recent tragedy had occurred.

On September 16, after our new supply of videotape arrived, we sailed out of the harbor at St. John's. By now, temperatures in Newfoundland had dropped considerably, and even in the daylight hours it was warm only when the sun was not behind the clouds. So no one was unhappy about returning to the Gulf Stream. As it turned out, however, we were heading into rough weather, and for several days the ship rolled and pitched. During the worst of it, waves washed onto the stern, and unattached objects in our cabins slid and crashed to the floor.

As we headed southeast, we had no way of knowing how valuable these extra dives would become. Until now, we'd explored only the first-class areas of the ship with the ROVs, but on our return trip, we expanded our mission and ventured into places no divers had ever reached before: third-class cabins, crew's quarters, and one of the doctor's offices, among others. We also found more unexpected artifacts, including the faux fireplace in Bruce Ismay's parlour suite,

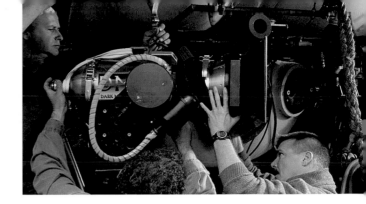

(Opposite) After towing out the MIRs, the *Koresh* heads back to the *Keldysh*. (Right) Jim Cameron's brother Mike, at right, inspects the housing on the 3-D camera mounted on the front of *MIR-1*. (Below) An aerial view of the launching of *MIR-2* over the side of the *Keldysh*. Looking like spider's legs, the various cranes stand poised over the ship's sides. A separate crane launches the MIRs, the Zodiac and the *Koresh*.

and a well-preserved bowler hat belonging to Henry Sleeper Harper of the New York publishing family, who had seen the iceberg pass by his window on the night of the disaster. In some of the areas we had previously explored, we were surprised by the sight of new, ghostly clouds, which looked almost like underwater smoke. Lori described these as "biological gelatinous masses." If the ROV were to perforate one, she said, the mass would eventually heal.

Since the weather by now was fine and clear, the dive schedule became much more aggressive. For four straight days the MIRs went into the water, with Jim and his brother Mike diving each time. The few hours between dives were packed with activity, as each trip had to be planned in a much shorter time than usual. The ROV team literally worked through the night to make sure Jake and Elwood were always ready to perform the next day.

(Left) Tabletops, probably knocked off their cast-iron bases when the ship struck bottom, lie in the debris of the third-class open space where passengers danced just hours before the collision. (Opposite) This green medicine bottle, with its contents still sealed inside, was discovered in the crew surgery just forward of the well deck.

Unfortunately, although Elwood was taken on some of the dives, he never functioned properly again. On the first attempt, his battery died on the way to the bottom, emitting bubbles for about ten minutes. Mike explained that these bubbles were extremely hot and could crack or rupture a sub porthole if they touched it, killing everyone inside. Genya worked to reposition the MIR so that the bubbles floated away from it, while Ken made it a point not to look out of his porthole until the danger had passed. On another occasion, Elwood made it safely to the ocean floor, but for some reason would not function and was forced to stay inside his garage for the remainder of that dive.

I did not make any more journeys down to the wreck, but while the MIRs were away, some of us headed to Mission Control to look at the footage from each previous day's dive. As Jake moved carefully through the forepeak and into the steerage and crew areas, we saw rooms that no one had laid eyes on since 1912. The large third-class open space under the forward well deck, like the first-class Dining Saloon, still contained table bases rising out of the silt and muck. Near one wall, the remains of tabletops rose up, apparently knocked off their bases when the ship struck bottom. The deadlights (the metal porthole covers) were all shut. Someone had obviously taken the precaution of closing them prior to the sinking.

Farther down in the bow were third-class cabins, their

walls also gone. We expected to see metal bedframes, but in these particular berths, none was found. At one point, Jake faced Scotland Road, the long E-deck corridor that stretched from one end of the ship to the other and was used by both crew and passengers to travel from the bow to the stern. Unfortunately, being inside the *Titanic* wreck can be extremely disorienting, and it was especially easy for the divers to lose their bearings in this part of the ship. Among the disjointed ruins, Jim and his brother did not realize they had found Scotland Road, so they did not send Jake down the companionway. This was a particular disappointment for Jim, since he had hoped to explore it.

In some ways, the area under the forepeak, at the very tip of the bow, was my favorite part of the newly explored sections. More of it was intact than other areas of the wreck because it had flooded gradually during the sinking, and its steel walls had not decayed. It was here, also, that Jake performed most brilliantly. He and Elwood had been designed especially for a place like this, their small size and maneuverability allowing them to squeeze into tight spaces and to explore narrow corridors and doorways.

The *Titanic*'s forepeak contained rooms for the crew. One was marked "Surgery" on the deck plan and proved to be the office of one of the doctors on board. Navigating gingerly so the hinge screws still in the doorframe would not snag on Jake's wire mesh, the 'bot was sent into the room to

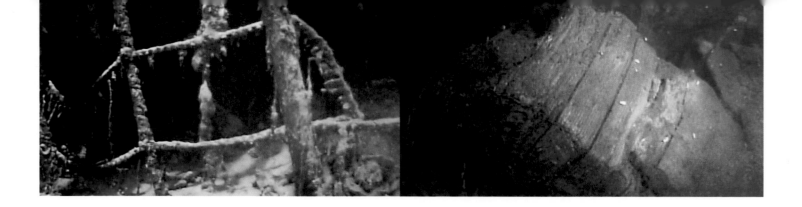

peer around. The built-in desk was still in place, its drawer handles clearly visible. Along the walls were shelves, and beneath the silt we made out the remains of medicine bottles. One was a bright green that looked entirely out of place against its drab surroundings, and we could see a white substance inside beneath the black rubber stopper. It seemed to be waiting for one of the ship's medical personnel to come along and give the remedy to a crewman.

Nearby, Jake explored a hospital room — a small cabin with two metal bunks and a single, wall-mounted washstand. The closed wooden door still remained in place, but the center panel had deteriorated enough so that Jake could squeeze through without difficulty.

Farther forward were the circular stairways — one for climbing, the other for descending — that passed through all the decks and led right down to the boiler rooms. The Firemen's Mess was at the top, their quarters were on decks farther down, and they worked in the very bottom of the ship. As a result, the men spent a lot of time climbing up and down those winding stairways. The stairs were narrow and could not have been easy for a novice to navigate — and they were definitely too cramped to risk sending Jake down them. At the top of one of the stairs, however, the 'bot sent back an image of a lone bottle, which looked as if it had once held beer, even though alcohol was forbidden. Although the firemen's quarters were hardly luxurious, Thomas Andrews,

who oversaw much of the ship's design, showed special care for his workers. When Jake discovered a drinking fountain near the stairs, we thought it probably had been installed there on Andrews' special instruction.

As Jim and Mike approached the starboard edge of the forepeak, they saw two doorways standing side by side.

"The first should lead into the Firemen's Mess," said Jim.

Inside the mess, the outside wall angled sharply, reflecting the shape of the hull at the bow, and the bases of tables rose out of the silt and fallen rusticles. But there were no visible remains of the kits and belongings the firemen had stacked there when their rooms had begun flooding below.

One of our goals was to descend into the cargo hold to look for the brand-new Renault that Philadelphian William E. Carter had been bringing to America. As Jake approached that section, he sent back images of strangely different rusticles hanging from the beams that crossed the cargo hatch. They were longer and more needle-like than the others, and whenever one was dislodged, it descended like a spear down into the depths. Then Jake wound his way down to the Orlop Deck, the second from the very bottom of the ship. It was here that the deck plans showed storage space for motorcars. We did find huge masses of cargo, including a stack of books or some other paper materials, but most were unrecognizable. Along the outside walls were batten boards, to which cargo had been tied to keep it from

(Opposite, left) A still-intact railing surrounds one of the ship's cargo hatches. (Opposite, right) This stack of what could be British newspapers or magazines was one of many cases being shipped, although its container has long since deteriorated. (Below) Among the heaps of intriguing debris-covered objects seen on the Orlop Deck was this wicker crate, probably used by steerage passengers (right) to transport their worldly belongings.

In the nearly two decades since the *Titanic* was discovered, the thinner metal of the top decks has deteriorated noticeably. (Inset) In this painting by Ken Marschall, which shows the remains of the gymnasium when Robert Ballard explored the wreck in 1986, only a single hole was present in the starboard Boat Deck. (Right) Today, a section farther along the Boat Deck has collapsed and fallen through in several places.

shifting. One particularly large mound could have concealed the lone automobile aboard. I thought I saw a lantern, like the ones used as headlights at that time, and something else was curved like a fender, but I would be exaggerating to say that it was definitely the Renault.

Although our explorations had so far revealed an astounding number of intact items that no one had seen since 1912 — beds, washstands, mirrors, the leaded-glass windows — much of the ship itself had deteriorated considerably since its 1985 discovery. On one dive, Jim planned to enter the first-class rooms on the upper decks of the stern section. But when the MIRs arrived, the divers discovered that just a few feet below the Boat Deck lay the portholes of C Deck, with only twisted metal between. Both the Boat Deck and A Deck had collapsed onto B Deck. Genya told us that this had occurred only in the last few years.

This was not the only deterioration we discovered over the course of the expedition. In order to create his present-day paintings of the ship, Ken had studied footage of the wreck since its discovery, and he was very aware of the changes over the years. The most noticeable seemed to be around the Boat Deck and A-deck areas. In the former, huge holes had opened up — some adjacent to the bulkheads, or walls, which told us they were not caused by the landing of submersibles. Some of the paneling in the gymnasium was

still intact, but its roof had collapsed, and the entire room had tilted down into A Deck. Bulwark railings at the bridge had fallen, and the walls of the officers' quarters were giving way. At one time, underwater explorers could catch only a faint glimpse of Captain Smith's bathroom, but it was now open, the remnants of the outer wall lying on the deck. Many windows along the A-deck promenade, through which Madeleine Astor and other first-class passengers were passed to the lifeboats, had disintegrated — especially where the metal between the windows was particularly thin. As Lori studied the rusticles, she theorized that much of the destruction to the *Titanic* had taken place only in the last few decades as the bacterial communities had grown exponentially. For much of the time the ship had been on the bottom, she thought, it had been in relatively good condition.

On these last dives, Jim also did some cleanup. Using the cutting mechanism on Jake, he severed much of the fiber-optic tether that had been strung around the exterior of the ship on the previous dives. This way, if anyone were to visit the *Titanic* in the next year or so before the tether had fully decomposed, it would be less visible.

On September 23, Ken, Mike, Jim, and Bill set out for the stern section — where two reciprocating engines still tower, in Jim's words, like "twin sphinxes" and a pair of gigantic propellers lie in the sand. But most of the stern, as Mike put it, is a "tangled, twisted mess. After a very short time," he said, "there was something in me that just wanted to get *away*....It's a *very* scary place....It *feels* like death."

Before they left the stern, Jim placed a bronze plaque there to honor the people who had died in the wreck. "The fifteen hundred souls lost here still speak," it said, "reminding us always that the unthinkable can happen, but for our vigilance, humility and compassion." Over the last seventeen years, the ship has received plaques from different expeditions, and most identify those who left them. But the plaque Jim placed on the wreck is anonymous — a memorial to the victims and to no one else.

On September 24, we went out on deck to watch the MIRs return. It was the last time we'd stand at the rail and scan the dark ocean for a glow of lights to appear suddenly below the surface. As the subs, the *Koresh*, and the Zodiac were being hauled in, many of us gathered at the stern for a brief memorial ceremony. Lori had made a small wreath and Jim began by describing the attacks of September 11 as a wake-up call for the twenty-first century — just as the sinking of the *Titanic* had sounded an alarm for the Western world almost a century before.

After the ceremony, a few of us went over to the port railing to watch the ocean. The sky was clear, and a brilliant half-moon shone above us, its reflection shimmering off the still, dark ocean. Suddenly, not fifteen feet away, we spotted a pod of dolphins darting about and leaping through the air. They were escorting us from the site just as they had on September 12.

The following afternoon, as we were reviewing footage in Mission Control, word came around that a white rainbow had appeared off the stern. We dashed out on deck, and beyond the pathway of churning water stretching out behind the ship, we saw a huge crescent in the sky — a band of what looked like snow-colored fog arching over the ocean in the direction of the *Titanic*. As we steamed toward Canada, we were touched by the benevolence of that final image. Unlike the multicolored rainbows that appear as portents of hope and new beginnings after a storm, this white arch hovered over the water like a ghost.

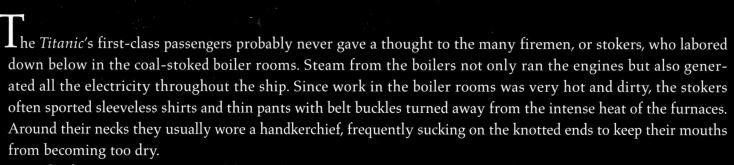

The *Titanic's* first-class passengers probably never gave a thought to the many firemen, or stokers, who labored down below in the coal-stoked boiler rooms. Steam from the boilers not only ran the engines but also generated all the electricity throughout the ship. Since work in the boiler rooms was very hot and dirty, the stokers often sported sleeveless shirts and thin pants with belt buckles turned away from the intense heat of the furnaces. Around their necks they usually wore a handkerchief, frequently sucking on the knotted ends to keep their mouths from becoming too dry.

The firemen were segregated from other crewmen; their quarters were all in the forepeak, deck upon deck, with their own mess room, washrooms, and showers. As many as fifty-four men would bunk in one room. Two circular staircases, one going up and the other down, connected them to the bottom of the ship and from there through

While passengers in all classes relaxed and enjoyed the voyage, firemen labored below to keep the boilers fired and the engines powered (depicted above in this scene from the *Ghosts of the Abyss* film). (Left) At the Belfast shipbuilding firm of Harland and Wolff, massive boilers are nearly ready to be installed. (Opposite) The boilers, once located deep inside the ship, are now visible at the aft end of the bow section. As the water pressure mounted during the two-and-a-half-mile plunge to the bottom, the faces of the boilers were pushed inward.

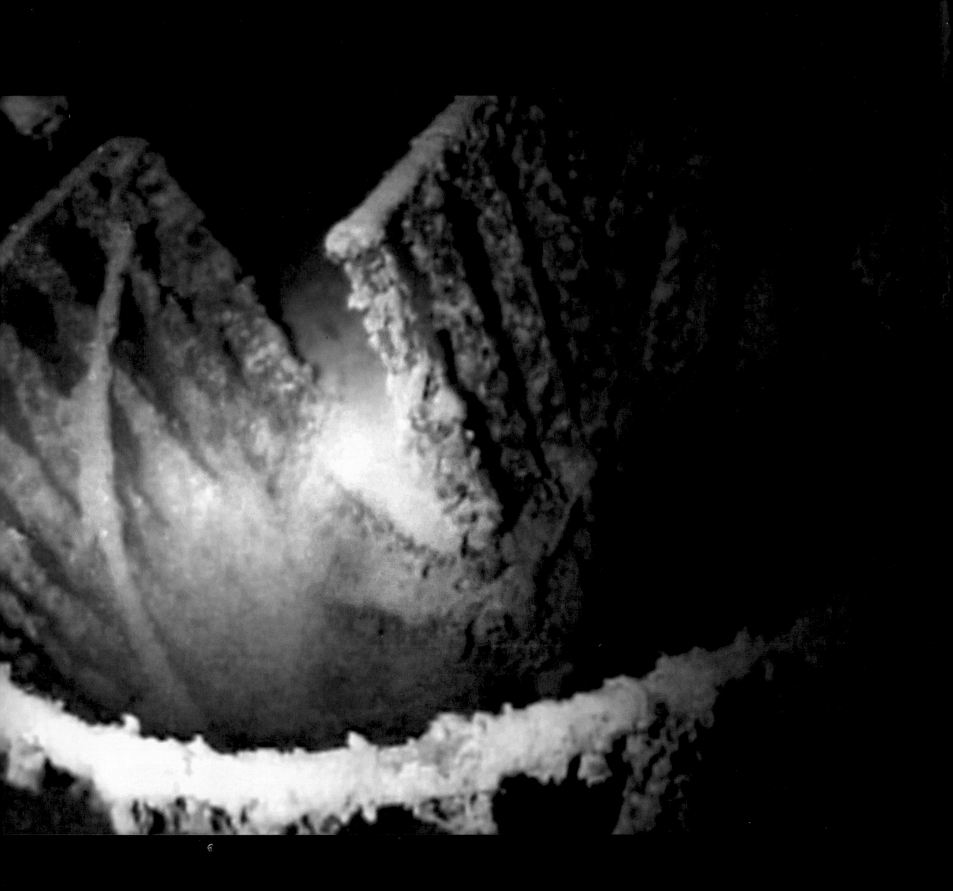

a passageway to the boiler rooms. "It was damned hard work," fireman George Kemish would write over fifty years later. "It was hell."

"They surely were a grimy, wiry, disheveled, hard-looking lot," first-class passenger Jack Thayer wrote of the stokers who were huddled with him on overturned collapsible B after the sinking. But the lifeboats would prove to be a great social equalizer. In boat No. 6, Molly Brown of Denver wrapped her sable stole around the legs of "a half-frozen stoker, black and covered with dust." In boat No. 13, twelve-year-old Ruth Becker handed out blankets she had brought from her stateroom to some of the firemen who were so thinly clad. Colonel Archibald Gracie, also on collapsible B, found the firemen and other crewmen around him to be offensively uncouth. But he quickly changed his feelings when one of them inquired as to the religion of everyone, and then led them in the Lord's Prayer.

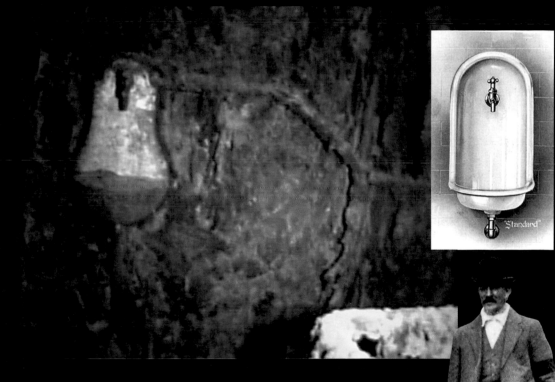

(Opposite) The circular staircase, its handrails still in place but unused for nine decades, began at D Deck and ran all the way to the bottom of the ship (left). It provided access from the firemen's quarters directly to the boiler rooms. (Above) At the top of the staircase stands the drinking fountain designer Thomas Andrews had thoughtfully installed for the use of the firemen. (Inset) A similar fountain from the period for use on board ship. (Right) Fireman Charles Hendrickson, who survived in lifeboat No. 1.

The *Titanic*'s bronze propellers were the largest on any vessel at the time, the two outboard ones measuring over twenty-three feet in diameter. Although the aft end of the stern section slammed into the sea floor with such force that it buried itself almost to the top of the rudder, the outboard propellers can be seen today (left) because the "wings" to which they are mounted were wrenched upward. (Below) A worker, barely visible at first glance as he stands at the stern of the *Olympic*, demonstrates the massive scale of the propeller blades.

The *Titanic*'s two sets of four-cylinder triple-expansion reciprocating engines (opposite, inset) were some four stories tall and the largest afloat. Each provided about 15,000 HP while turning the wing propellers at 75 RPM. When the ship broke in two, the two forwardmost cylinders fell out and landed in the debris field, while the other three on both the port and starboard sides remained fitted in the stern part of

the ship. (Above) Today, these monuments to Edwardian engineering stand exposed at the forward end of the stern section, towering above the sea bed "like twin sphinxes," as James Cameron described them. (Left) Deep within the engine room are the massive columns supporting the starboard intermediate-pressure cylinder. (Inset, left) An engine before installation. (Opposite) The cylinder atop the port high-pressure engine was knocked out of alignment, a testament to the powerful forces that tore the vessel in two.

In Fairview Cemetery

As we approached the opening to the harbor at Halifax, a naval ship and a Canadian Coast Guard vessel cruised toward us. At first I thought they were there to protect us, but before long I realized they were protecting themselves from us. We were no longer just researchers and filmmakers; we were foreigners on an alien ship, docking in threatening times.

We had chosen to land in Halifax instead of St. John's because it was on the Canadian mainland and connected to rail service, which could take many of us back home if the airlines were still grounded. Our *Titanic* expedition had lasted much longer than we'd expected, and despite telephone and Internet connections, we felt extremely isolated. We were all eager to get back to our families and friends.

Before we dispersed to our separate destinations, however, some of us went with Jim to Fairview Cemetery, one of three in Halifax where nearly one hundred and fifty victims of the *Titanic* disaster are buried. As Jim began filming us in these burial grounds, nothing appeared unusual at first. Celtic crosses and domes marked the taller monuments, and a slight breeze ruffled the clumps of leaves that had fallen among the graves. But the rows of more familiar-looking headstones gave way to a field of short, gray marble markers and a sign that identified them as graves for victims of the *Titanic*. Many in the group were taken aback by these bare memorials and their numbing uniformity, but Lori was especially shocked that many bore no name — only a number representing the

sequence in which the body had been recovered. These passengers had not been identifiable, and here they had been laid to rest, nameless casualties of a great ocean tragedy.

As we mourned their shortened lives, we also grieved for those who had died at home while we were at sea. They, and the lost passengers and crew of the *Titanic*, were all very much alive to us. Only days before, we had entered rooms where some of these people had lived. We had viewed artifacts two and a half miles beneath the ocean's surface that had not been seen or touched for nearly ninety years — a glass on a washstand, a piece of tattered cloth flung over the headboard of a bed, a woman's high-laced shoe — all haunting traces of the lives of those who now lay silent all around us.

When Jim had embarked on this expedition, he'd trusted that there were new discoveries to be made inside the lost liner. But nothing had prepared him, or any of us, for the number of relics that spoke so eloquently of the people who had made and used them: finely rendered leaded-glass windows still intact, hand-carved wood moldings showing the marks of the craftsmen who'd created them, White Star dishes unbroken and neatly stacked in a fallen sideboard. And over all, the vestiges of corridors and promenades, the echoes of Edwardian elegance, and our memories of the people who had laughed, dined, prayed, and died in that doomed but magnificent ship.

We had just added another chapter to the story of

the *Titanic,* and even as we prepared to leave, I dreamt of returning to the wreck one day to discover more of the *Titanic's* secrets and to help commit them to film, so millions more could enjoy their splendor and thus honor the memories of the people they represented.

On my last day in Halifax, as I was returning to the *Keldysh* after a brief on-shore visit, I found myself walking beside an older Russian crewmember from the ship. His cabin had been near mine, and as he apparently spoke no English, we had only nodded hello each day. Once again we greeted each other, and then, very slowly and carefully, he struggled to ask, "What city…?"

"Los Angeles," I replied.

And then, again, very slowly, he said, "You… come… back!"

I hope I do.

133

TITANIC: *Then and Now*

Within the many hours of digital footage shot during the *Ghosts of the Abyss* expedition lay images of scores of objects that evoked the liner in her prime. Here is a selection of *Titanic* artifacts — matched with photographs that strip away the rust and decay to reveal them as they once were.

(Below) The bases of tables still stand in the third-class open space on D Deck. The same cast-iron base can be seen (inset, left) on this small table used in a third-class or crew bunking room.

(Left) The brass letters affixed to the oak paneling in the A-deck elevator lobby are still legible. (Inset) A similar sign from three decks below stands behind a potted palm.

(Below left) A rusting ladder mounted on the windbreak of the first-class entrance on the Boat Deck matches the one seen behind Captain Smith on the *Olympic* (inset).

(Right) A railing once used by third-class passengers on their way from the open space below the well deck down to E Deck is matched (inset) in this photograph of a similar third-class stairway.

(Below) The forward davit arm for lifeboat No. 1, which stands today on the starboard Boat Deck. (Inset) An advertisement for the Welin Quadrant davits that were used on the *Titanic*.

(Above) A composite of images taken by *MIR-1* shows the exterior of the starboard A-deck promenade. The same area can be seen below the lifeboat in the inset (left).

(Right) A crystal decanter from the Dining Saloon, identical to the one inset, lies in the debris field.

(Below) Hemp rope remains on this boat-launching bitt. It was looped here (inset) while lowering a lifeboat on April 15, 1912.

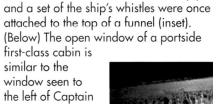

(Above) This section of waste-steam pipe and a set of the ship's whistles were once attached to the top of a funnel (inset). (Below) The open window of a portside first-class cabin is similar to the window seen to the left of Captain Smith (inset).

What Happened When the *Titanic* Sank?

James Cameron has lived every *Titanic* buff's dream — from making more dives to the wreck than anyone else to actually reenacting the disaster using full-scale movie sets.

From these experiences, he has formulated a number of intriguing theories about the foundering of the ship and its descent to the ocean floor.

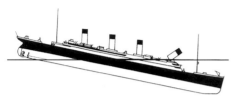

Why did the first funnel fall?

During the filming of the movie *Titanic*, huge windstorms struck the film set in Baja, Mexico. "I always thought I was going to drive up one morning and see a funnel missing," recalls Cameron. Yet despite these high winds, the four funnels on the *Titanic* set remained in place, much as smokestacks on real ocean liners do during storms at sea. Why, then, did the *Titanic*'s forwardmost funnel suddenly fall as the ship was sinking? Why did the others not fall at the same time?

The funnels were held in place with stays — thick cables that stretched from the upper part of the smokestacks down to the Boat Deck. During the liner's last moments, crewmen struggled to free the two collapsible lifeboats that were stored atop the officers' quarters below the first funnel. They managed to drop the boats to the deck but were unable to put them in davits for launching. In reenacting this during filming, the director discovered that the stays blocked the paths of the two collapsibles to the davits. In attempting to get these boats launched, perhaps First Officer Murdoch or Second Officer Lightoller severed or somehow detached a few of the stays that held the first funnel.

Previously, it was assumed that the expansion joint just aft of the first funnel widened so much during the sinking that the stays snapped — and the funnel, leaning forward by then, toppled. However, the funnels were elliptical, and thus more likely to fall to the side than forward. Moreover, as the liner nosed downward, the angled funnels actually stood more upright, increasing their balance. "The funnel is dead vertical at the moment it's supposed to have fallen," says Cameron.

What most likely caused the forward smokestack to fall were the severed stays, and the weight of the water that began pressing against the funnel's base as the bow dipped under. The sides apparently crumpled, since the wreck shows the trunking below the funnel to be bent inward. As the ship was listing to port at the time, it likely toppled in that direction. And since Murdoch, working on the starboard side, was farther along in launching collapsible A when the ship plunged, he was more likely than Lightoller to have cut the funnel stays from that side.

The stays may also have been responsible for sweeping many of the lifeboat davits off the Boat Deck. During the plunge to the bottom, the remaining funnels also detached — yet the stays, strong enough to hold the funnels in place during a storm, likely remained connected. As the ship sank, the light, hollow funnels would have acted like parachutes and followed more slowly. The stays attached to them would then have been swept aft along the deck, ripping the davits from their bases. This would explain why a number of davits lie tangled in a heap on the ocean floor.

Did the Grand Staircase float away?

Another mystery concerning the wreck is the loss of the entire Grand Staircase from the relatively intact bow section. Jim Cameron has explored to the bottom of the stairwell, and no traces of the heavy oak handrails or of the many wrought-iron balustrades remain. When the staircase set created for the filming of *Titanic* was flooded, the entire staircase was dislodged. Could the same thing have happened on the *Titanic*? As the ship was plunging, first-class passenger Jack Thayer, swimming nearby, saw something rise out of the water which he assumed was the bow of the ship brought up by trapped air. Clearly it wasn't, but could it have been the staircase instead? Seaman Joseph Scarrott testified at the British Inquiry that lifeboat No. 14 had rescued a crewman who "was on top of a staircase. It seemed to be a large piece of wreckage anyhow which had come from some part of the ship. It was wood anyhow. It looked like a staircase."

What happened to the bow section?

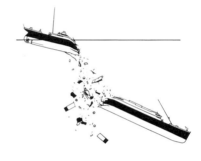

After the *Titanic* broke in two, the bow section continued downward and forward. The mast was forced back, probably shattering the wooden bridge and wheelhouse. Water flooded down the corridors of the officers' quarters, and the forward walls of the deck house were splayed out.

The bow section descended at an angle and struck the bottom at a point underneath the forepeak. As the nose buried itself, the mass of the larger section from the bridge aft forced the entire bow section down. Mud was pushed up from all sides, and a huge stress was placed just forward of the superstructure. Internally, massive destructive forces were at work. The ship compressed, causing decks to push down onto one another and the ship to bulge out on either side. This is obvious inside, where columns, particularly on D Deck, are bent like knees. The compression created by hitting the bottom forced water out of the *Titanic*, rupturing the sides below the well deck and knocking the tabletops outward off their bases in the third-class open space.

The steel cover over the No. 1 cargo hatch was also apparently blown off by the water being compressed out of the ship. Once free, it was carried forward and appears to be the only sizable piece of debris in front of the bow.

Today the wreck is still under tension, bent as it is with stress on the decks and the hull. Jim Cameron does not claim to have all the answers for what happened as the *Titanic* sank. "It's a complicated geometry," he says. "We may never know all of it."

The compression that occurred when the bow section hit bottom bent interior columns (left) and blew the steel cover of the cargo hatch (right) off the Forecastle Deck.

INDEX

BIBLIOGRAPHY

Beesley, Lawrence. *The Loss of the Titanic.*
    London: William Heinemann, 1912.

Booth, John, and Sean Coughlan. *Titanic: Signals of Disaster.*
    Westbury, England: White Star Publications, 1993.

Bullock, Shan F. *A Titanic Hero: Thomas Andrews, Shipbuilder.*
    Riverside, Connecticut: 7 C's Press, 1973.

Gracie, Colonel Archibald. *The Truth About the Titanic.*
    New York: Mitchell Kennerley, 1913.

Jack's Reference Book For Home and Office.
    London: T. C. & E. C. Jack, 1912.

Lightoller, Commander Charles H. *Titanic and Other Ships.*
    London: Ivor Nicholson and Watson, 1935.

Lord, Walter. *A Night to Remember.*
    New York: Henry Holt & Company, 1955.

Lynch, Don. *Titanic: An Illustrated History.*
    New York: Hyperion, 1992.

*Ocean Liners of the Past: The White Star Triple Screw
    Atlantic Liners Olympic and Titanic.*
    Cambridge, England: Patrick Stephens, 1970.

Oldham, Wilton J. *The Ismay Line.*
    Liverpool: Charles Birchall and Sons, 1961.

O'Donnell, E.E. *Father Browne's Titanic Album.*
    Dublin: Wolfhood Press, 1997.

Parisi, Paula. *Titanic and the Making of James Cameron.*
    London: Orion Media, 1998.

Tarrant, D. R. *Marconi's Miracle.*
    St. John's, Canada: Flanker Press, 2001.

U.S. Senate, Subcommittee Hearings of the Committee on
    Commerce, 62nd Congress. *Titanic Disaster.*
    Washington, D.C.: Government Printing Office, 1912.

Walton, Thomas. *Know Your Own Ship.*
    London: Charles Griffin and Company, 1918.

Wreck Commissioners' Court, Proceedings before the
    Right Honourable Lord Mersey, on a Formal
    Investigation Ordered by the Board of Trade into the Loss
    of the S.S. "Titanic." 1912.

MAGAZINES: *Engineering, Harper's Weekly, Popular
    Mechanics, Titanic Commutator, Woman's Own*

NEWSPAPERS: *Bismarck Tribune, Bournemouth Daily Echo,
    Detroit News, Hollywood Reporter, Minot Daily News,
    New York Times, Portland Oregonian, Seattle Post-
    Intelligencer*

WEBSITES

Encyclopedia Titanica
    www.encyclopedia-titanica.org

James Cameron's *Titanic* Expedition 2001:
What We Saw on and inside the Wreck, by Ken Marschall.
    www.marconigraph.com

Titanic Inquiry Project
    www.titanicinquiry.org

All at Sea with Dave Gittins, by Dave Gittins
    www.users.senet.com.au/~gittins

Bridge Duty: Officers of the RMS *Titanic*, by Kerry
Sundberg and Inger Sheil
    www.geocities.com/Athens/Delphi/2622

ORGANIZATIONS

British Titanic Society
    P.O. Box 401
    Hope Carr Way
    Leigh
    Lancashire WN7 3WW
    England

Titanic Historical Society Inc.
    P.O. Box 51053
    Indian Orchard, Mass. 01151-0053
    USA
    www.titanichistoricalsociety.org

PICTURE CREDITS

Every effort has been made to correctly attribute all material reproduced in this book. If any errors have unwittingly occurred, we will be happy to correct them in future editions.

Unless otherwise indicated, all color photographs and computer graphics images © 2003 by Walden Media, LLC. Used by permission of Walden Media, LLC, from the *Ghosts of the Abyss* 3-D movie. All paintings are by Ken Marschall unless otherwise stated.

BB   Brown Brothers
BTSA   Booth-Titanic Signals Archive
CE   *The Cork Examiner*
DLC   Don Lynch Collection
FBC   Fr. Browne SJ Collection
ILN   *Illustrated London News*
KMC   Ken Marschall Collection
NMR   National Monuments Record, U.K.
UFT   National Museums and Galleries of Northern Ireland, Ulster Folk & Transport Museum

Endpapers: Vancouver Maritime Museum.
Cover: Title treatment by Concept Arts.
5:      FBC.

CHAPTER ONE
12: Peter Christopher.
13: FBC.
14: (Left) FBC. (Right) Merseyside Maritime Museum.
15: (Top) UFT. (Insets top and bottom, and far right) KMC.
17: (Top) Courtesy of Jeremy Nightingale. (Bottom) BB.
18: (Left) FBC. (Right) CE.
19: Robert D. Ballard.
20: (Top left and top right) *The Sphere*/KMC. (Bottom left) Byron Collection, Museum of the City of New York. (Bottom right) National Maritime Museum/KMC. (Inset) KMC.
21: (Left) BTSA. (Middle) BB. (Right) FBC.
22: (Top left) BB. (Top middle) DLC. (Top right) Private collection.
22–23: (Bottom) ILN/KMC.
23: (Top) KMC.
24: (Left) *The Shipbuilder*. (Right) George Behe Collection.
27: *The Sphere*/KMC.
28: (Left) Parks Stephenson Collection. (Right) BTSA.
29: Mariners' Museum.
30: DLC.
32: (Left) Courtesy of Randy Bryan Bigham. (Middle) ILN/DLC. (Right) New York Public Library.

CHAPTER TWO
37: Don Lynch.
38: (Right) Don Lynch.
43: Charlie Arneson.
44: Don Lynch.

CHAPTER THREE
53: (Inset) KMC.
54: (Top) UFT.
55: (Inset, bottom left) BB. (Inset, bottom right) KMC.
56: (Top left) ILN/KMC. (Top right) FBC.
57: (Insets, top and bottom) UFT. (Bottom left) ILN/KMC.
58: (Bottom left) BB. (Bottom right) FBC.
59: (Inset) UFT.
60: (Top left) FBC.
64: (Top) NMR/UFT composite photo.
65: (Inset) Peabody Essex Museum.
66: (Inset, top) Library of Congress. (Inset bottom) BB.
68: (Bottom and inset left) KMC.
69: (Top right) NMR.
70: (Top) UFT.
71: (Top right) National Maritime Museum. (Inset) BB.
72: (Inset, top) NMR.
74: (Left) Library of Congress. (Inset left) UFT.
75: (Left) National Maritime Museum.
76: (Inset) KMC.
78: (Bottom) KMC.
80: (Inset) KMC.
81: (Inset) NMR.

CHAPTER FOUR
88: (Right) Don Lynch.

CHAPTER FIVE
96: (Top) CE. (Bottom) Courtesy of Jeremy Nightingale.
98: (Top left) KMC. (Top right) *The Shipbuilder*.
100: (Bottom middle) Byron Collection, Museum of the City of New York. (Bottom right) Titanic Historical Society.
101: (Top) NMR.
102: (Top) NMR.
103: (Top) CE. (Inset) BB.
104: (Inset left) NMR. (Inset right) Courtesy of Akzo Nobel/ Photo by Ken Marschall.
105: (Inset bottom) NMR.
106: (Left) Courtesy of Randy Bryan Bigham. (Right) NMR.
108: *The Sphere*/KMC.
110: (Inset top) UFT.

CHAPTER SIX
119: (Top) Bettmann/CORBIS/MAGMA.
122: (Left) CE.

CHAPTER SEVEN
124: (Bottom) UFT.
127: (Left) UFT. (Inset) 1911 Standard Baths and Plumbing Fixtures catalogue, Miller and Anderson Collection, Handley Regional Library, Winchester, VA. (Bottom) ILN/DLC.
129: (Inset) UFT.
130: (Inset) UFT.
131: (Inset) UFT.

EPILOGUE
132–133: Peter Christopher.

TITANIC: THEN AND NOW
134: (Insets, bottom left and top left) KMC. (Inset, top right) UFT. (Inset, bottom right) National Maritime Museum.
135: (Insets, top left and middle right) KMC. (Inset, top right) Peabody Essex Museum. (Inset, middle left) *The Sphere*/KMC. (Inset, middle center) BB. (Inset, bottom) ILN/KMC.
136: Ken Marschall.
137: (Middle) Ken Marschall.

Prints of Ken Marschall's artwork are available from Trans-Atlantic Designs, P.O. Box 539, Redondo Beach, CA, USA, 90277. www.transatlanticdesigns.com

ACKNOWLEDGMENTS

I would like to thank a number of individuals whose assistance has been invaluable. First and foremost, of course, is Jim Cameron — who made it all possible and whose support of the book has been greatly appreciated. Ed W. Marsh of EarthShip Productions, with his encyclopedic knowledge, has never failed in providing information and answering the innumerable questions sent his way. I also want to acknowledge the following participants in the expedition for filling in the pieces when my notes, memory, and knowledge failed me: Adrian DeGroot, Jason Paul, Belinda Sawyer, and Eric Schmitz. Others to whom I am grateful are George Behe, Randy Bryan Bigham, Claudia Huerta, Ed Kamuda, and Elizabeth Stanton.

I am extremely grateful to those survivors of the *Titanic* disaster who left written, privately published accounts: Karl Behr, Washington Dodge, Marie Jerwan, Elmer Taylor, and John B. Thayer. I am particularly indebted to the following passengers, unfortunately no longer living, who so willingly shared their memories and stories: Olaus Abelseth, Bertram Dean, Ruth Becker Blanchard, Washington Dodge, Jr., Edith Brown Haisman, Edwina Troutt MacKenzie, Eileen Lenox-Conyngham Schefer, Nelle Snyder, and Winifred Quick Van Tongerloo. Finally I would like to acknowledge *Titanic* survivor Millvina Dean, for sharing her story and her dear friendship.

— *Don Lynch*

Thank you, Jim, for your great vision and friendship, without which I never would have experienced this fantastic voyage. My gratitude to Parks Stephenson, for his exhaustive analysis of the Marconi suite video and for providing direction for those cutaway illustrations and creating certain components; to Ed Marsh, the "anchor" of EarthShip, for a thousand favors; to Ellen O'Brien for her expert assistance with image enhancements; to Adrian DeGroot and Stephen Pavelski of the EarthShip computer graphics department for their fabulous renders of the Reception/Vestibule areas and Grand Staircase, respectively; to Al Lopez at Creative Logik Universe, LLC, and to Mike Enriquez of CLU for his stunning Marconi/Silent Room renders; and to Claudia Huerta and Justin Shaw for their quick turnarounds with all those hundreds of image grabs.

— *Ken Marschall*

Madison Press Books would like to thank James Cameron for his introduction and Ed W. Marsh and his team at EarthShip for countless favors. Special thanks are also due to: Debbie Kovacs at Walden Media; T. Kenneth Anderson at Ulster Folk & Transport Museum; Edwin Davison of Davison & Associates; Rebecca Ebert of the Stewart Bell Jr. Archives; Chuck Comisky; Randy Bryan Bigham; Jeremy Nightingale; and Kathryn Dean.

MEMBERS OF JAMES CAMERON'S 2001 EXPEDITION TO THE *TITANIC*

ABOARD THE *KELDYSH*

Lewis Abernathy
Ron Allum
Charlie Arneson
Dennis Baxter
John Bruno
Mike Cameron
Jim Cameron
John David Cameron
Todd Cogan
Adrian DeGroot
Piet De Vries
Anton Floquet
Alan Gitlin
Mark Goodwin
Daniel Greenwald
Dale Hunter
Andy Johnson
Lori Johnston
George Kallimanis
Jeff Ledda
Don Lynch
Michael Maltzman
Ken Marschall
Ed Marsh
Barbara Medlin
Pat Miller
Tim Murphy
Vince Pace
Sven Pape
Jason Paul
Bill Paxton
Charlie Pellegrino
Gig Rackauskas
Marc Robinson
Rich Robles
Belinda Sawyer
Eric Schmitz
Kristie Sills
Tava Smiley
Kathe Swanson
Andrew Wight
Randy Wimberg

Special thanks to Genya Cherniev, Anatoly Sagalevitch and all the *Keldysh* crewmembers.

ABOARD THE *MT EAS*

John Broadwater
Mark Heinrich
Corey Jaskolski
Ben Kinnaman
Peter McKibbin
Russell Passmore
Tom Prince
Steven Saint-Amour
Ralph White

Editorial Director: Hugh Brewster
Associate Editorial Director: Wanda Nowakowska
Project Editors: Hugh Brewster and Wanda Nowakowska
Manuscript Editor: Kathryn J. Dean
Editorial Assistance: Imoinda Romain
Art Director: Gordon Sibley
Graphic Designer: Jennifer Lum
Production Director: Susan Barrable
Production Manager: Sandra Hall
Image Enhancement: Ken Marschall, Ellen O'Brien, Colour Technologies
Visuals Liaison: Ed W. Marsh
Computer Graphics: EarthShip Productions, Creative Logik Universe
Printing and Binding: Eurografica

GHOSTS OF THE ABYSS was produced by Madison Press Books,
which is under the direction of Albert E. Cummings.

Created in cooperation with 🔵 WALDEN MEDIA